P9-EEP-768

SISTER KAROL'S
BOOK OF SPELLS
AND BLESSINGS

*

PRESENTED TO

_____

BY

_____

DATE

_____

SISTER KAROL'S
BOOK OF SPELLS
AND BLESSINGS

HYPERION

NEW YORK

SISTER KAROL'S

BOOK OF SPELLS

AND BLESSINGS

*

Karol Jackowski

*

*

*

*

LIBRARY OF CONGRESS CATALOGING-IN-PUBLICATION DATA

Jackowski, Karol.
    [Book of spells and blessings]
    Sister Karol's book of spells and blessings / by Karol Jackowski. — 1st ed.
       p.   cm.
    ISBN 0-7868-6772-8
    1. Spiritual life — New Age movement.   2. Magic. 3. Ritual.   4. Prayers.   I. Title: Book of spells and blessings.   II. Title.
BL624 .J3 2001
291.4'32 — dc21   2001016813

Book design by Richard Oriolo

FIRST EDITION

10 9 8 7 6 5 4 3 2 1

CONTENTS

INTRODUCTION

THIS IS A BOOK ABOUT prayer and how important ritual becomes at certain times in our lives. At least in the life of nearly everyone I know. Even those who are decidedly not religious (though by no means unreligious), find the occasional need to pray, to ask for divine inspiration and intervention. And they too feel the specific desire to do so through prayers and rituals. They too believe in prayer's power to help make good things happen. This kind of nonbeliever lives at the heart of what the Dalai Lama sees as a spiritual revolution of sorts: One that doesn't find its inspiration in organized religion, but in a level of concern about one's spiritual life and the well-being of others. ✳ While these nonbelievers may hold in contempt the Gods of organized religion (especially those made in the image and likeness of their believers), many find themselves drawn simultaneously to a mysterious presence moving through the days of their lives. Never an abstraction, this is a sacred presence that surrounds, inspires, and guides. It is felt as soulful, often religious, and experienced as divine. The call to prayer is deeply personal and altogether universal, and the human longing for ritual profound. At some level, we all share a desire to live close to our God. ✳ The spells and blessings you'll find in this book are for believer and nonbeliever alike. There are some favorite rituals for believers in God, Jesus, Mary, angels, and saints, as well as what I very fondly call spells: heartfelt, homemade prayers for those who find a spiritual presence in nature, neighbor, and the ordinary matters of everyday life. In all of these spells and blessings you'll find a little of both—the deeply personal mixed with the deeply traditional—always the most powerful prayer of all. It's the matters of the heart, when put into some ancient ritual, that the Gods seem to find most irresistible. ✳ Long before religion became organized (and its powers centralized), practicing religion at home was the norm. Everybody did it. Every household had its Gods, its altars, and its daily religious rituals. All of life and everything that happened became part of ritual prayer. I found ancient religious texts full of household spells and blessings for the most ordinary things, such as heal a foot, silence a barking dog, prevent snakebite, have a good singing voice—and a personal favorite—make a man tongue-tied. ✳ At first, some of those concerns appeared trite and unworthy of divine attention; until I read on and on to see how

✳

sacred ordinary everyday life was to our earliest ancestors. These commonplace rituals were all folk medicine for the soul, all meant to strengthen their connection to the divine mysteries of everyday life. All of life is holy and everything that happened became part of their life's mystery. Long before Gerard Manley Hopkins ever wrote the poem "God's Grandeur," our earliest ancestors discovered that the world was indeed "charged with the grandeur of God." Now those are what I call the good old days. ✳ There's no official explanation of why the earliest prayers were called spells, except for the primitive belief that that's exactly what Gods do when we call—stop by for a spell. The spell itself has everything to do with God's visit and what happens when that kind of divine intervention occurs. Those who engage in such spells do so in times of crisis as well as with the ordinary matters of everyday life. And because such rituals come from the soul, they are naturally experienced as divine. Lives are somehow changed by such mysterious activity. Even if we don't immediately get what we want, something happens, and what we want to happen gradually becomes real. That's the power of spells and blessings, and therein lies the magic. It changes our life. ✳ The fact that I'm now fifty-four years old, with a Ph.D., and still possessed by an enchanted spiritual life has occurred with relatively little effort of my own. I owe it all to the Catholic Church. Every

Catholic I know grew up with a mysterious vision of life because life itself was full of mystery from the very start. Long before the age of reason, we learned from nuns and priests ("God's representatives") about our three-in-one God, the Trinity, made up of a Father, a Son, and a Holy Spirit—known by us for years as the Holy Ghost—the most mysterious of the three. As one God, they created everything, most especially us. ✳ Then there was Holy Mary, Mother of God and our Mother; as well as Virgin Mother of Jesus, Son of God; and spouse of Saint Joseph. Following the Holy Family were all the choirs of angels, cherubim and seraphim, plus the entire communion of saints. From the very start we knew for sure that we were not alone. ✳ Most mysterious of all, were the daily Holy Communion rituals. The Latin Mass with candles, incense, booming pipe organ, and Gregorian chant—all building up to the goose-bump experience, the moment of consecration when ordinary bread and wine become divine, become the Body and Blood of Christ. From Grade One forward, a very important part of Catholic education consisted of daily Mass and Communion. And now, as a result of receiving the sacrament daily for years, whenever I look at bread and wine, I always see something different. ✳ There were also other dramatic religious devotions that required our grade school attendance—litanies, novenas, Forty Hours' Devotion, Benediction,

May Crowning, Living Rosaries, Stations of the Cross—all of which became important annual events on the Church calendar, and in our daily Catholic lives as well. All of which also became important parts of us. Mix all of the above together for a lifetime and it becomes you. Then mix all of that with half a lifetime of the daily prayers and rituals in being a nun, and it becomes you even more. At least it totally became me. So much so that it now became this book. ✳ All the soulful questions I've ever been asked, and all the prayerful requests I've ever received, all help make up this *Prayer Book of Spells and Blessings*. Rarely does a day go by that I don't receive at least one request for prayerful support. Like those ancient household spells, the subject matter is as ordinary and diverse as passing a test, selling a painting, finding an apartment, blessing a baby, or winning a contest—altogether ordinary requests for divine intervention. ✳ Most want to know the prayers and rituals that mystified me in the beginning, as well as favorite novenas and prayers to saints known to grant specific favors. More and more are also drawn, as am I, to the prayers and rituals of other religious traditions as well. All feel called to practice religion at home and all find themselves at home with the universal appeal of all religious rituals. Such are the spells and blessings that you'll find here. Something, it is hoped, for everyone. ✳ Far more than just a little religious recipe book however, here you'll find everything you need to make up your own *Book of Spells and Blessings* —the most important book of all. Here, in Part One: Spells and Blessings 101, some thought is given to explaining the impulse or the call to pray; what it is, where it comes from, and what to do when we hear it. ✳ Because creating sacred space is one of the first things to do, here you'll also find some common elements of sacred spaces and be encouraged to build your own home altars and shrines. Nearly all I know who hear the call to pray, nun or not, also hear the "holy altar call." They all have some sacred spot where they light candles and make wishes. And they all keep their personal treasures there as well. And if you've been drawn to pick up this book, in all likelihood you already have at least one altar or shrine at home. ✳ At the heart of this book, an attempt is made to understand the magic of ritual, and how it changes our lives. Everything we experience is capable of being transformed, of being lived in a different way, and religious rituals help free and enable us to do that. Questions of where the power of ritual comes from, as well as why, when, where, and how to ritualize top the list. Here you'll find the common elements of ritual prayer, as well as a seven-step process on how to create your own spells and blessings. Step by step by step is how it all happens. Slow and steady is how the magic in ritual works. ✳ In Part Two of this book, Spells and

Blessings: Mine, you will find old and new rituals for nearly every occasion. Some reflect ancient Christian rites, while others draw on rituals that predate Christianity. Some are purely Catholic in origin (but known to work for all), and others integrate valuable insights from nontraditional, "New Age" experiences. And some are just pure and simple fun. ✳ All responded at one point in time to someone's prayerful request. All reveal the mystery and magic I know and love in the rituals of Catholicism. All contain the pure joy and fun I know and love in the rituals of my family, sisters, and friends. And all offer opportunities to taste and see for yourself how divine, how comforting, how mysterious, and how much fun ritual prayer can be. ✳ The greatest hope in all of this is that you, the prayerful reader, will begin here and now to put together your own *Book of Spells and Blessings*. A pure heart, a longing soul, and an inquiring mind are all you need. Where and when do you notice the impulse and hear the call to pray? What do you do to get in touch with the Gods? How, when, and where do you find divine activity? That's the place where all spells and blessings begin. ✳ There's even some sacred (blank) space provided in the end for you to get started. The thought of a bazillion *Books of Spells and Blessings* makes me think our world would be far less a mess if that happened. All that energy focused on letting good things happen through us. That's the magic stuff of which miracles are made. That's the divine stuff that can change us and the whole world. ✳ In any event, and in the end, I pray that this *Book of Spells and Blessings* will do for you what it did for me—allow you to taste and see how divine the experience of this life can be, even in its darkest, most devastating, most confusing, most mysterious moments. I pray that this book blesses you with peace. And with everything else you want.

SPELLS AND
*
BLESSINGS 101

THE CALL TO PRAY

THE CALL TO PRAY IS and is not as mysterious as it sounds. It's such a mysterious impulse because it always comes from something in life that moves us profoundly and always feels like it comes from God. And yet really, in a way, it's not at all that mysterious, because it happens to so many of us, and not infrequently. As a matter of fact, the longer I live the more frequent and ordinary the call to prayer becomes. ✳ Practically every day I meet someone who hears the call and wants to know what to do. Something happens, it doesn't take much, and the need arises for divine assistance, inspiration, protection, comfort. Being called to pray is just that ordinary and just that mysterious at one and the same time; heard by believer and nonbeliever alike, and in a language understood by all. Now how mysterious is that? ✳ The call to pray always feels 100 percent mysterious to me, regardless of its frequency. The ordinary manner of the call only enhances and magnifies the mystery as far as I'm concerned. In the beginning of my Catholic education, I was somehow led to believe that every twinkle in the starry, starry night was a heartfelt prayer on its way to God. Clear evidence to me that billions of people heard the call to prayer. That's how extraordinarily ordinary it is. We were also told that the end of this world would come when every star found its way to that divine resting place where all prayer is answered: God's lap. ✳ Every star a prayer. I still find myself automatically believing this almost every night when the single, solitary star passes through a piece of sky in the kitchen window of my two-room New York City apartment. Only one star is visible in the night sky over my neighborhood, leading me to believe that this is a great spot to have prayers answered. The success rate appears exceptionally high. And as far as I can see, we only have one big unanswered one (the size of a planet) left up there. ✳ All of that goes to show that I'm clearly not alone when it comes to the divine, primitive-feeling impulse we have to pray— whether it be to heal, console, get pregnant, get money, get a job, pass a test, sell a house, get rid of a headache, or find true love. Requests like that I hear daily. And every time I see how moved so many are to punctuate life's most stellar, most painful, most confusing, even most ordinary moments with prayer, I always feel like that starry-eyed belief is not so silly. It's not just me. And it's not just a nun thing. It's not so silly to see how such simple, soulful prayers would quite naturally feel like twinkling specks in the night being drawn toward God. "Such stuff as dreams are made on."

THE CALL TO RITUAL PRAYER

❋ Because the call to pray is as ordinary and personal as it is mysterious and divine, it's rarely difficult to see where it comes from. Something noticeable happens to confuse us, delight us, hurt us, and if we take care to listen before leaping, we naturally feel the impulse and hear a call to look for or pray for divine assistance. And whenever we run into life's greatest mysteries along the way—accidents, natural disasters, illness, death, hatred—the call to ritual prayer is one that comes to us then just as well. ❋ Such soul-stunning experiences often reduce us to silence and highlight our helplessness. They also leave us wanting to do everything we can to turn things around, to transform such difficult situations into gateways that lead to new life. It's life itself that calls us to ritual prayer, and life itself that invites us to enter into and partake of its transforming powers. ❋ The moment of greatest grace always lies in taking care to listen, in keeping still whenever we become overwhelmed. Such untimely stillness is always good because it helps us see what's going on, and always shows us, in the end, what to do next, even if nothing. The call to ritual prayer always sounds like that in the beginning. It's prelude lies in stopping, looking, and listening for the still, small voice, for some insight and understanding into what's happening. The key is always to remain calm. Or, as I once wrote to 1,500 college students in a directive on emergency residence hall procedures, "The key is to remain clam!" The key to the heart of any mystery is always to remain clam. ✳ Everyone I know who feels called to personal prayer also feels called to ritual prayer, to nourishing more profoundly the capacity to let good things happen through them. In the depths of our soul, I believe all are born with a call to be mediums of love and kindness. We all have it in our power to shape fate by the choice to let either loving and just or hateful and destructive things happen through us. Whenever anything moves us, how we respond is the most fateful act of all. In that way, the future does not appear to be all that mysterious. In that way, the future is created by the way we respond to things right now. Yikes. How scary is that. ✳ At any given moment, we do things that either lift one another up or put one another down. We can be kind and generous, or mean and selfish. Judgmental or accepting. Forgiving or not. Everything we do works to create or destroy the sense of goodness in life, the experience of peace on this earth, and most important, a good night's sleep. Every choice we make serves to unite or divide; to make others and ourselves better or worse, more or less socially conscious. The God-given choice to be or not to be is now and ever shall be, moment by moment, ours, all ours. Such are the makings of destiny, and such are the workings of ritual prayer.

✳ Whenever we hear the call to pray, we can be sure that the impulse comes to serve one purpose only, and the call comes to lead us to one true thing: nourishing the capacity to let only good things happen through us. The call to pray is always a matter of becoming our very best self, of seeing more clearly and loving more dearly, day by day. If we are not more kind, more understanding, more patient, more loving, and more fun to be with as a result, then it's probably not prayer we were called to. And it certainly wasn't God making the call. How do we know? "By their fruits," is what Jesus suggests, by the way they live their life, by how loving they are toward one another.

✳ There's also a noticeable kind of awakening that occurs when a call comes from God. We begin to see things differently. We experience a change in consciousness that often results in some greater understanding, some insight, a sense of perspective and humor. We may see something now that we didn't notice before. Feel more patient and less impulsive, less moved by anger. The awakening that comes with a call from

God is always a matter of becoming more loving, more forgiving, and more generous human beings. If the call comes truly from God, it can be a call to nothing other than awakening all of godly love and goodness born deep in the soul. ✳ For many of us, the call to ritual prayer, like the call to personal prayer, came very early, and persisted throughout life. In addition to beginning every grade school day with Mass and Holy Communion, in my Catholic high school and college, we also prayed at the beginning and end of every class. Year by year, we learned more and more of the mystery and magic of religion, and year by year we experienced more and more the mystery and magic of prayer, particularly ritual prayer. Along with higher and higher education, we also got higher and higher religion. ✳ Never isolated activities, however, all of those ordinary Catholic rites and rituals became part of everything we did, eight hours a day, five, sometimes six days a week, for years. That's why even "lapsed" (non-churchgoing) Catholics are the first to admit how strange it is that some things never leave them. They still feel Catholic no matter how out of line they are with the Church. When it comes to religious development, some things become part of us forever. That's how powerful prayer and ritual can be. ✳ Nearly every Catholic I know, for example, still has a secret heartfelt devotion to God's Mother, Mary. Marian devotion was cultivated in us (especially girls) from day one in Catholic school. In the early 1950s we learned of children our age in Lourdes, France, really being visited by Mary and really receiving messages from her. And we really believed it could happen to us as well. All the girls in my grade school (Saint Stanislaus in East Chicago, Indiana) belonged to the Children of Mary, a Catholic-school church group that nourished a personal devotion to the Mother of God and focused on convincing us of how divine it was to remain a virgin until marriage or death. ✳ All I remember about being a Child of Mary was that we processed into church on the first Sunday of every month (and on feasts of Mary) robed in white and blue. We wore knee-length white capes with a pale "Blessed Mother" blue Peter Pan collar, and the same color blue felt beanie with a white satin "M" in front and a silky white string tassel on top. Because of the outfit and the procession I also remember feeling spiritually special. One of Mary's girls. For many of us such devotion deepened and didn't disappear over time. And for many of us such heartfelt devotion to Mary also had a lot to do with our gradually finding out how divine it is to be a woman. ✳ Daily we heard of strange, incredible miracles happening to ordinary people who subsequently became saints. The Gospels are full of such miraculous stories, as is the history of the Catholic Church. We all believed in miracles (as does 80 percent of our current population), and we were all urged strongly to pray at home, especially at the beginning and end of every day, and before and after every meal (which is also believed to prevent food poisoning). ✳ Most prayed in private with rosaries, prayer books, statues, candles, and novenas. Some did so more publicly, praying aloud together as a family. I've always been a strong follower of the Gospel method of prayer—go to your room, close the door, and pray in secret, keeping in mind that God always knows your need far better than you do. (Keeping that in mind also makes me wonder what the purpose is in praying out loud and in public.) ✳ In discovering the mystery and magic in ritual prayer at an early age, we were also introduced to ritual's strangely powerful ways and means of drumming up divine activity. While growing up Catholic was always a highly ritualized religious experience, those sacred rituals were never confined to Church alone, but were brought home just as well. Ours was a religion that reached beyond church right into our homes, right into our daily lives. For me, such homespun folk rituals had long-lasting effects. ✳ As though it happened just last January, I can still envision the Three Kings House Blessing, the first Catholic ritual that really hit home, no pun intended. Every year on January 6, Feast of the Three Kings, the parish priest and two altar boys visited all Catholics (and some nonCatholics) in the neighborhood to bless their homes and families at the beginning of the New Year. ✳ The priest knocked on the door three times and it was very important not to keep him waiting; as though it would be a sin or bad luck if he had to knock three more times. Father entered the house first, wearing a floor-length gold cape, and holding a small black prayer book with both hands. Two altar boys followed: one holding the holy water, chalk, and white cloth, the other swinging the censer back and forth, creating thick, swirling clouds of burning frankincense and myrrh. Such was the setting in which the Three Kings House Blessing took place. ✳ The priest began the ritual by reading a brief prayer of blessing on us and our messy house, which always gave us goose bumps. He then covered the four corners of the living room with incense and sprinkled us (including dog, parakeet, and turtle) with holy water, which always made us laugh. Exchanging the prayer book and the holy water wand for the chalk and the white cloth, the priest and altar boys then walked back to the door. With the white cloth, the priest rubbed away the chalk markings from the previous year, and wrote in its place K+M+B+1952—the first-name initials of the Three Kings (Kaspar, Melchior, and Balthazar) plus the New Year. ✳ The fresh chalk markings concluded the ritual and signaled the moment for a token of thanks. Someone, usually a parent, slipped the priest an envelope, after which the three departed in a cloud of smoke, to repeat the same ritual, house after house after house. I now know that every religious tradition has its own House Blessing ritual, making it one of the most powerful rituals we know. Apparently the Gods love to make themselves at home, love to stop by for a spell, love to abide within, love to be part of the household and its activities. Gods love to live close to their people. ✳ In addition to being initiated into the prayers and rituals of Catholicism at a very young, very impressionable age, those of us who grew up in an ethnic neighborhood also practiced that kind of folk Catholicism, consisting mostly of powerful little rituals for everyday matters. Calling on Saint Anthony with a special rhyming prayer would always help find lost items. Burying Saint Joseph in the backyard (or basement) would help sell or buy a house. And when faced with the impossible we prayed to Saint Jude. ✳ Our neighbor in East Chicago got everything she ever asked for with the Novena to the Infant of Prague. Saint Michael protects everyone from fire, and if you walk into any fire station, you'll surely find Saint Michael. Then above and beyond them all was this: If you don't get an answer from God always go to Mary, God's Mother; even if (as in the feast at Cana) you run out of wine at a party. Mary turns down no one. It was even believed that she sneaks sinners into heaven under her big triangular skirt. All the above are proven true time and time again. And all are reflective of a spiritual life that helps get the faithful through difficult times, giving them a peace over which awful circumstances have no power. ✳ Many homes I knew had some little obscure prayer space set aside, a self-made shrine or altar tucked in a corner or on a dresser top, usually tended to by the woman of the house. Some families built serious, high-maintenance yard shrines, usually tended to by the man of the house. Both were clear indicators of how typical it was for us to take religion into our own hands, so to speak; how natural it was for us to engage in some kind of personal ritual or prayer whenever necessary, and at our convenience. ✳ For most of us, ritual prayer was just a simple, unnoticed, ordinary part of everyday life. We too had our household Gods and altars, and practicing religion at home was normal, not at all strange. Everybody did it. Religious rituals were mixed in with family rituals, which were mixed in with neighborhood life. Plain and simple, rituals naturally become reflective of who we are. ✳ That being the case, we come to know instinctively when the time calls for ritual prayer. There are certain times in life that naturally beg for divine intervention and the powerful blessing that religious rituals hold. Most religions celebrate and ritualize seven such extraordinary moments; seven of life's turning points worthy of the oldest, most divine rituals we know: Birth, Forgiveness,

Communion, Adulthood, Marriage, Priesthood, Sickness, and Death. High holy rituals that effect what they signify. All religions and their believers are held together, sustained, enriched, and mystified by their rituals. And most of us experience very early in life just how mysterious, powerful, and life-changing religious rituals can be—even sacramental. Divine activity actually occurs—oftentimes giving us goose bumps and making us laugh—always leaving us in peace: An inner peace that, over time, becomes nearly impossible to disturb. ✳ In the days of our lives, less momentous occasions may also call us to ritual prayer. Wanting a new job will do it, as will beginning or ending a relationship, or moving into a new apartment. Endings and beginnings are always powerful turning points, and almost always bear calls to ritual prayer. Sometimes confusion will warrant a ritual for clarity, and almost always, a ritual of gratitude and thanks is the only way to express pure joy. If the occasion is a momentous one for you, and if you feel the need to respond in some special way, then the call you hear may very well be to ritual prayer—to drum up a little divine activity of your own. It all begins with the call. The moment most full of grace, mystery, and magic is the call to invite the Gods in for a spell and pray for a blessing.

THE HOLY ALTAR CALL

IT'S ONLY NATURAL WHEN WE hear the call to pray that we also feel the need to create sacred space where that can happen. That's what the holy altar call feels like, the need to prepare a place for divine intervention to occur. And when it comes to home altars and practicing religion at home, there is clearly nothing new under the sun. It's been going on since the beginning of time. The need to create sacred space is so deeply embedded in the human soul that its origins far predate any organized religion. ✳ Long before religion ever got organized, our ancestors communed daily with the Gods at home. In every culture throughout history and the world, home altars and household gods and goddesses are found. Sacred space was created within the home for the deities to abide and reside there as well. All I know who hear the call to pray also hear the holy altar call. Like our ancestors, they too feel the need to create a sacred space at home, a divine door and threshold through which the Gods can enter and stay for a spell, a holy place within which the Gods can abide. ✳ In every religion, altars mark the spot where divine intervention occurs, in much the same way we honor as sacred those places where significant events happen. It's not unusual to see white crosses along a country roadside where someone died in an accident, or mounds of flowers and burning votives at the scene of some tragedy. Not long ago, on my way to work, I noticed what looked like an art project in the trash at the curb. It was an icon of the Virgin Mary sur-rounded by red velvet, decorated with gold braiding, and mounted on a piece of plywood. I removed it from the trash and stood it up against a nearby fence. If it was still there at the end of the day, I had every intention of making it mine. ✳ Well, it was still there at the end of the day, but I didn't dare make it mine. It appeared as though, throughout the day, passersby had transformed the divine trash into a streetside shrine. Small bundles of fresh flowers—tulips, daisies, and wilted roses—were propped up on either side, and two seven-day votive candles—one blue, one white—burned in front. There were three pennies near the candles, as though wishes were made there; and an empty beer bottle, leading me to believe heartfelt prayers were offered there as well. Clearly, I wasn't the only one who stood in awe of the trash day transformation. And to this day I still cannot walk by that same spot without remembering and hearing a call, though faint and small, to bow my head and remember. Even on the streets of New York City, and even on trash day, the holy altar call can be heard loud and clear. ✳ In the beginning, whenever someone built an altar, it was always in response to God who had just visited there. It was to mark that spot as holy, as sacred space, as somehow qualitatively different than any other space. Something extraordinary happened there, some divinity appeared, making that spot holy, marking it as a sacred place where divine intervention occurred. And if God visited there once, it's entirely likely that God will visit there again. Ordinary space all of a sudden becomes enchanted, magic, sacred. All of a sudden we're standing on holy ground. ✳ All altars, including home altars, are sites of great religious significance. They serve both as a door for Gods to enter and intervene, as well as a dwelling place where Gods can abide. Altars reveal how the holy is imagined and present in the home, marking the spot where divine activity occurs. That sacred place may be a dresser top, windowsill, bookshelf, fireplace mantel, nightstand—any place where we can welcome and receive divine intervention. The holy altar call is nothing more or less than finding a place and creating a space where Gods, angels, and saints can make themselves at home in our home; where all holy spirits, including deceased family and friends, can stop by and sit for a spell.

FINDING A SACRED PLACE

When it comes to finding sacred space in the home for spells and blessings, following your gut instinct is always the best you can do. Along with millions of others, you may also find, as I did, the oriental art of feng shui helpful in choosing a place and divining a space for your altar. Whatever place you choose draws spiritual energy into your home and your heart, and finding that divine spot, or spots, is the very first step. ✳ Because most home altars develop spontaneously, over time, you may already have found the most sacred spaces in your home, and may already have begun to assemble there objects that hold special meaning and significance: photographs, seashells, statues, candles, rocks and stones, incense. No place or space in the home is inappropriate for an altar. And the more often you feel called to ritual prayer, the more places you'll find where divine activity occurs. ✳ Some find the entranceway to the home is the best place for an altar. And some religious traditions, like Catholicism, Judaism, and Buddhism, have rituals for entering and leaving the home. For example, it's an old custom among Catholics to bless themselves with holy water and a Sign of the Cross. My Jewish neighbors kiss their fingertips before rubbing the mezuzah in the doorway for a blessing. Doorway blessings are some of the most ancient rituals we know, marking entranceways as perfect spots for altars and shrines. ✳ Many also find, as I do, that the bedroom is the best place to create sacred space. Gods and angels have a reputation for visiting us in sleep and dreams, and a bedroom altar extends that invitation nightly. Bedroom altars also offer a unique kind of privacy and protection that living rooms, dining rooms, and entranceways often do not. I for one find that exclusive kind of privacy and protection essential for personal and ritual prayer, though that's not its only blessing. Facing the altar at the beginning and end of every day is also believed to energize and comfort the spirit in us and in our home. Being surrounded by sacred stuff naturally makes us feel better. ✳ Over the years, you too may find, as I did, that you now have several home altars. One main, all-purpose altar, and several side altars dedicated to a specific purpose: one honoring deceased relatives and friends, the mermaid shrine in the bathroom, the new baby side altar, the votive stand for the wishes of those who visit, and a doorway shrine to bless all comings and goings. All appeared over time, as the spirit moved, and all were created to mark and bless the place where divine activity occurs.

CREATING SACRED SPACE

Once you've found the sacred place for your altar, the next step is to create the sacred space. In creating my sacred spaces, I found it both natural and helpful to consider the following: placement of the altar, purifying the space, and assembling sacred objects. It's the fine mix of all three that takes ordinary space and makes it sacred. And it's by the power of those three that our homes become dwelling places for our Gods. Altars everywhere is enough to make me feel better, nearly indestructible at times. There is no doubt that you too will find the same to be true in creating your sacred space. They are divine sources of strength and fountains of youth. ✳ In considering the placement of the altar, you may find it helpful to consider the direction you want to face: east, west, south, or north. Associated with the rising sun, the east is the place of new beginnings and new life. If your life is aching for a new beginning, and your soul is longing for new life, then you may want to place your altar facing east. The south is often seen as the place of growth and expansion. So if you feel your life is in need of wider, more open spaces, then facing your altar toward the south may be most fitting. The west, land of the setting sun, is the direction to face when transformation and change are needed in your life. And facing north, as my altar does now, puts us in touch with the direction of the soul and the deepest, most mysterious dimensions of life. Whatever direction you align yourself with for the placement of your altar serves to draw that specific directional energy into your life and your home. So in creating the space for the placement of your altar, consider carefully the direction toward which your life is drawn. ✳ Purifying or cleansing the altar is the next step to consider in creating your sacred space. In the Catholic ritual of Eucharist, Mass, and Communion, just before the time of consecration where bread and wine become divine, the altar is prepared and purified by being incensed. The priest adds frankincense and myrrh to burning coals and proceeds to incense the four corners of the altar, above, below, and all around. The priest then incenses the servers on the altar, who in turn incense the congregation and priest as well, all in preparation for divine intervention. ✳ In cleansing and purifying your altar space, you too are encouraged to do so with incense or a smudge stick (bundles of dried sage). Any incense can be used for this purpose, and smudge sticks can be either homemade or purchased anywhere ritual supplies are sold.

Whatever you find most natural and helpful is best. I use both, not only to purify new altar space, but also to clear the mind and prepare the soul, the inner altar, for prayer (as well as writing). And if you're allergic to smoke, holy water purifies and blesses just as well. Once you've found the place and prepared the space, you can then begin the deeply personal, totally spiritual process of assembling the sacred objects to be placed on your altar. ✳ What makes objects sacred? The energy from what happens around them, and in this case, the divine loving energy that surrounds them. It's when objects become saturated with the energy of what we love that they become holy. Objects that are loved and treasured naturally become sacred over time. So much so that we take every measure to ensure that our most sacred objects are passed on and cared for long after we're gone. And the longer objects are loved, cared for, and revered, the more sacred they become. It is most fitting then, that sacred objects from your personal life be kept and revered on your altar. ✳ Religious objects and images, because they have been worshipped and prayed over for centuries, some for thousands of years, naturally tend to be the most sacred of all. In the center of my main altar stands a nineteenth-century wooden carving of the Virgin Mary from the Philippines, found in an antique shop. She has no hands, and her features are worn smooth. Half the moon under her feet is gone, but the face of the angel holding up the other half is still there. The divine energy of being prayed to and loved for centuries is also still there, so much so I could feel it, I could hear her speaking. And in the words of my dear, deceased Auntie Lily (and much to the dismay of my Uncle Frank), "If it speaks to you, buy it." Which I did with reckless abandon. ✳ It's not at all unusual for us to be moved noticeably by religious art and images. Certain works of art naturally "speak" to us, and that kind of "speaking" is very much part of the nature of the holy. Because such images represent a vision of the sacred, it's quite natural that they move our Holy Spirit and even inspire us to pray. The face of Buddha moves millions to prayer, me included, as do icons of the Virgin Mary and other sacred works of art. If you're not sure what I mean, visit the Metropolitan Museum of Art in New York City—or any museum for that matter. Find the paintings of Joan of Arc and Mary Magdalene, sit there for a few minutes, then you will know for sure how naturally our souls are moved by art and how divine that feeling naturally is. ✳ Objects representing the divine power in nature—earth, air, fire, water—also belong on the altar. Those who know that this world is indeed charged with the grandeur of God do not find it hard to believe that all elements of creation are alive in some mysterious way. All are filled with the energy of what happened around them. Rocks and earth from Stonehenge, Jerusalem, any Holy Land or any sacred site naturally feel sacred to believers, while rocks and dirt from a shopping mall parking lot naturally do not (although I suppose some would find that debatable). In the good old days, stones were always worshipped as living embodiments of divine life, making them even more worthy to be kept on an altar. ✳ Walk through any flea market or antique store and you may find, as I always do, objects that "speak," things that bear the energy of previous owners, and either attract or repel us. The vibes are either good or bad. You either must have it or not. Because of the energy surrounding them, even the most ordinary objects can become qualitatively changed, can become a treasure. They too can become sacred. And they too belong on our altar. ✳ In the Catholic tradition, relics from saints were often minuscule pieces of cloth that touched the bones or burial place of one revered as holy. All of a sudden, just with a touch, ordinary cloth becomes sacred, becomes relic. We all share a desire to own a little piece of those whose lives move us so profoundly, so powerfully, so much so that even the smallest, most ordinary inanimate objects become alive to us in ways that feel sacred. ✳ By revealing something sacred to us, any object can become something else, something holy, even though its physical appearance remains the same. And for those who know religious experience, all of creation, all of nature is capable of revealing the sacred. Nothing is profane. No object is inappropriate for our altar if it holds for us the sacred. ✳ So personal objects, religious objects, and objects from nature all belong on our altar. A New York artist I know covered an upright piano with an altar cloth of handwoven fabric from Mexico—upon which were arranged fresh flowers, half-burned candles in assorted colors, stones and dirt from sacred sites visited, religious statues found at flea markets (and repainted), photos of loved ones (including art works she wants to sell), figures of aliens, and an empty pack of cigarettes. At the time she was desperately trying to quit. ✳ My altar is covered with hand-embroidered linens found at flea markets, upon which are three images of the Virgin Mary: the 200-year-old statue from the Philippines, and two folk art images of the Guadalupe Virgin from Mexico. Three votive candles are set in front, surrounded by rocks and dirt from Stonehenge, Easter Island, and other sacred sites; crystals, censer, holy water, fresh flowers; and a ceramic container with dirt and stones from the New Orleans grave of my grandmother and godmother. In front of an icon of the Angel of Kiev (made by a best friend) rests the first and last page of a manuscript a colleague is trying to get published; and on top of a little "Lucky Book Chair" (made by another best friend) rest the business cards of my agent and editor—all reflective of the sacred energies most active in my life right now. ✳ In assembling the objects for your altar, I encourage you to do the same. Put your life there, and surround it with the naturally divine elements of air, earth, fire, and water. Gather the objects most sacred to you and those you love and arrange them there as well. Your altar is you and represents what is most holy to you, your heart's desire. Let intuition be your guide, because therein lies the Holy Spirit of God, and all other kinds of divine activity. Once sacred space is created in your home, you too will find that the call to ritual prayer and divine activity becomes more frequent, a more ordinary part of everyday life. And before you know it, the call to engage in the magic of ritual will soon become your daily bread—the most divine way to begin, get through, and end every day.

THE MAGIC OF RITUAL

THE MAGIC OF RITUAL, LIKE the call to pray, is and is not as mysterious as it sounds. When something that we want to happen becomes real, that's the essence of magic. That's really what magic is. Something we envision becomes true. Yet getting what we want oftentimes doesn't seem to be anywhere nearly as mysterious as how it happened, how we got what we prayed for, how the magic of ritual works. That's the real mystery. That's the point at which we often look back, scratch our heads, and wonder what happened. What were the elements that came together to answer our prayer? What are the ingredients that make the magic of ritual work? As far as I'm concerned, in the deep, dark, unseen world of miraculous events, it just doesn't get much more mysterious than that. ✳ Einstein believed the most beautiful thing we humans can experience is the mysterious. And even though what we want may not become real immediately, or as soon as we wish, something still happens to us every time we pray. Even medical science is now beginning to recognize as true the amazing and mysterious power of prayer, once, twice, even three times removed. Praying for ourselves, our loved ones, and even those we don't know at all, somehow works. What we pray for actually happens. That's no big insight on my part or that of medical science. According to Jesus, if we do not hesitate in our heart, but believe what we say will happen, that will be granted us. It's that simple. "Whatever you ask for in prayer, believe that you shall receive, and it shall come to you." (Mark 11:23–24) ✳ So then why do bad things happen to good people? Why don't we always get what we pray for? Because in the words of the priestly Tielhard de Chardin, "We are not human beings on a spiritual journey. We are spiritual beings on a human journey." Bad things cross everyone's path, even that of God's only Son, Jesus, because it's all part of what it means to be human. That's life. Bad stuff happens. Pain, suffering, sickness, death, disappointment, tragedy, all happen to good and bad alike because it's part of the human journey. Part of the mysterious cycle of our lives. The miracle always lies in what we do when bad things happen to anyone. How we respond when awful and tragic things happen. How we get through the very worst of times. And this is where the magic in prayer most clearly does its work. ✳ Understanding what happens when we pray is the ultimate mystery. Divine activity occurs and we are moved in ways we most often don't see or feel, and certainly don't understand. Some kind of transformation occurs though. Something changes in us. We cannot sit for a spell with deities and walk away untouched, even though at times it certainly may feel that way. Those blank feeling times are what the saints call the dark night of the soul. Something's happening, but we are completely in the dark when it comes to understanding what that something is. So much so that it feels to us like nothing's happening at all, and what we want to happen will never become real. We'd even bet our bottom dollar that the sun will never come out tomorrow. ✳ But not all reality is physical and material, and not all power manifests itself in ways that we can see or control. The reality we're talking about here is spiritual, having to do with the inner life where outcomes can't be forced or controlled, no matter how good our intentions are. That's not how holy spirits work. This is the world of the soul, Innerland, where we mostly don't have a clue about how things work. And because spells and blessings draw us into that world, their magic works in soul time, spirit time, where hours, days, weeks, and years mean nothing. Those wheels of divine activity grind exceedingly slow but exceedingly fine, all the while showing us what great strengths patience, hope, and perseverance are. ✳

Whenever we pray, and whenever we engage in religious rituals, we enter into sacred space and place ourselves in the presence of God. Be there. While Jung assures us that "Bidden or not, God is present," it's we who tend to be nowhere nearly as present. Even so, what happens to us there, in the presence of God, does so in the places of the heart and the depths of the soul—all unfamiliar territory to us, and all very full of mysterious goings on. And it's in those depths that our life is changed every time we pray. ✴ What happens in the presence of God has everything to do with our being transformed and changed in some way, with our becoming more capable of living life differently—maybe kinder, more generous, braver, less angry, funnier. So even though we may feel like nothing is happening, and think that we're talking to ourselves, we are nonetheless moved quite profoundly in ways we don't always feel and hardly ever understand. That's the mystery of ritual prayer and therein lies its magic. Something happens to us every time we enter into sacred space for a visit with the Gods, even if we don't know or understand what it is. ✴ Because the magic of ritual lies in the fact that we are indeed transformed by such mysterious activity, something really does happen, an attempt is made here to understand what the elements are that converge to make that kind of magic. What is it that causes such profound transformations to occur? For every moment that's magical, there appears to be the right time, the right mix of ingredients, and the right constellation of elements to generate such divine activity. I found four things that like to happen together to make that kind of divine magic: the power in belief, the power in necessity, the power in nature, and the power in repetition. All four explain why, when, where, and how to ritualize, and all four always put me in touch with magic in ritual.

BELIEF

Everything I know and believe about the power in prayer and the magic in ritual comes from what I was told about Santa Claus years ago, and what I later found true in the Gospels as well: If you don't believe, you don't receive. Thoughts, desires, wishes, and prayers are all very powerful tools in the life of our spirit, and what makes their magic work is faith. Believing it all is the source and center of all spiritual life. It's the air holy spirits breathe, the life holy spirits cannot live without. If we really believe what we say will happen, with absolutely no hesitation in our heart, then what we ask for will indeed be granted us. Plain and simple, in words attributed to Jesus, "Let it be done to you according to your faith."

(Matthew 9:29) ✳ Jesus tells everyone who has a miracle; it's because of their faith that the miracle was done to them. And by the power in that kind of faith, if we knock, doors open, if we seek, we find what we're looking for, and if we ask, we really will receive everything we ask for. We may even receive, as I've discovered lately, far more than we ever ask for or imagine. Such is the amazing power in simple faith. And that's the reason caution is always advised in discerning what to pray for: Be very careful. You're going to get it. ✳ It's the hesitation in our heart that's the greatest obstacle to the kind of faith that moves mountains. And it's lingering doubt that drains the hope slowly out of any dream. While there's something about pure belief that may appear naive, childish, and foolish, like nothing more than wishful thinking on our part, it's just that kind of single-hearted belief that has everything to do with the magic of ritual. It's also just that kind of hesitation in our heart that's enough to break the spell. We must believe that we shall receive what we wish and pray for; giving no thought whatso-ever to how, when, and where our prayer should be answered. Always leave details to the deities. ✳ So great is the real power in faith that mountains can not only be moved, but apparently can also be lifted up and hurled into the sea (Mark 11:23). The point being that enormous obstacles can be moved out of our way by the power in faith. The most important ingredient in the magic of ritual, therefore, is the pure strength and confidence of our faith. It's the pure, simple power in belief that helps attract and welcome those outcomes for which we dearly hope and pray; it jump-starts and charges the magic in ritual. ✳ Faith's soul mate and helpmate in the magic of ritual is focus, focus, focus. Focus on what? On what we're asking for, what we're praying for. Be very specific in focusing your request, as specific as middle initials. And while focusing on what it is that we really want oftentimes ends up being far more complex than what seems obvious, two general rules apply. When it comes to aiming the power of your faith, harm no one, and focus on letting good things, and only good things, happen through you. ✳ The reason for focusing the power of our faith on what is good, right, just, and holy has everything to do with the natural law of karma: Whatever you put out there will come back to you, not only in kind, but ten times over. It also has everything to do with The Golden Rule of doing unto others as you want others to do to you; because what you do to others will indeed be done to you in time, for better or worse. It's a divine law of nature. Thus the everlasting caution to be very careful what you ask for. Never ask something for yourself at the expense of someone else. Ask instead, for example, that all obstacles be removed, clearing the way for your prayer to be answered. The most important ingredient in focusing the power of our faith is always love sweet love. Faith and love spark the real magic in ritual. They always bring out the God in us.

NECESSITY

When it comes to focusing the power in faith, we have only to look at our life and see what's going on. It's the pressure points, the sore spots, and the points of greatest inner tension that all hold the divine power in necessity. And even though they may all feel like hell on earth, inner tensions are often signs of divine activity breaking through. Gods have a long-standing reputation for appearing in storms, even causing them. Some were even known to throw lightning bolts. In Biblical days, and before, there were always creator Gods and destroyer Gods who governed the mysteries of life. And it's the divine energy of the latter who whip up storms in our lives as well. So while tensions and anxieties may feel more disturbing than divine at first, that's a divine sign for those who believe. That marks the spot of dire necessity, and it's there that we need to focus our attention and God's. The origin and starting point for all ritual is always our most personal experience, the joyful and sorrowful mysteries of our own life. ✳ So whatever and wherever our most urgent needs are, therein lies the divine power of necessity and its ability to transform us and the way we feel. Necessity is not only the mother of invention; it's also the mother of magic. Gods don't want offerings anywhere nearly as much as they want what's in our hearts and souls. That's the most important stuff in life. And that becomes the divine stuff of magic and miracles. ✳ In focusing on the mysteries in our life, we welcome divine intervention in a way nothing else does. That's how extraordinarily powerful personal participation is in making magic. It can't happen without us and the stuff of our lives. It's the condition of becoming deeply, personally involved that takes hold of us in sometimes startling ways, strengthening our connection to the unseen, undone, mysterious side of everyday life. Whether it be the pain and sadness of loss, the bewilderment of confusion, or the pure joy of dreams come true, the magic in prayer always comes from the joyful and sorrowful mysteries of our life. It always has everything to do with the inner necessity in our heart's most urgent desire. Never underestimate the potential magic hidden in necessity. ✳ So when it comes to focusing the power in faith, always begin with what's happening in your life. Wherever the happening places are, so too are the makings of magic. Moments of bewilderment, bad news, tension, good news, pain, all put us in touch with the deepest mysteries of life. The way life unfolds rarely coincides with our expectations, and whenever that happens, we can be sure that divine activity is at work. Bad news and misery are mysterious facts of life that always throw us into a state where we naturally cry out of the depths for help, and naturally feel the need for divine intervention. Focus the power in faith on any mystery of your life, put that divine stuff on the altar, and let the magic in prayer do its work. ✳ Whatever it is about the mysterious workings of faith and necessity, one thing we know for sure: Its power to summon the Gods is both extraordinary and magical. Why? Because wherever we find inner tension, and whenever we experience dire inner necessity, there it is that the work of transformation has begun. That's what transformation feels like in the beginning. Something in life is disturbed, maybe ending, and maybe ending badly in our eyes. That's where we notice the need for something to change, for something to happen, for some kind of divine intervention to alter positively the way we feel and the course of our life. Endings are always starting points for some kind of new life, full of the kind of divine energy that even causes resurrections from the dead. That's also where ritual prayer does its best work in changing minds, hearts, and souls in a way nothing else and no one else can. As far as I'm concerned, that's magic, pure and simple.

NATURE

✳ The kind of transformation and change we experience in the course of our lives is altogether like those changes and transformations we witness in nature, year after year after year. As a matter of fact, it is so much the same that the divine power in nature, being as charged as it is with the grandeur of God, became the determining factor in setting the dates for organized religion's high holy days. The primitive belief behind the synchronicity of nature and religion is that if we align ourselves with the cycles of nature, the seasons of the year, and the phases of the moon, we will increase significantly the divine power in our prayers and rituals. ✳ Our earliest ancestors even believed that their spells and rituals were necessary to help turn the seasons of the year; to help transform summer into fall, fall into winter, winter into spring, and spring back into summer again. They believed it was the divine power in their prayer that kept time moving. Since the beginning of time, the power in the seasons of nature has always been a divine ingredient in creating the magic of ritual. ✳ It's no accident or coincidence, therefore, that Christians celebrate Christmas and Jews celebrate Hanukkah at the time of the Winter Solstice, the longest night and shortest day of the year. It's the "O Holy Night" wherein light overcomes the dark and the season of increasing daylight begins. Associated in nature with the birth of the Sun, that holy season was designated by the early Christian Church as the birthday of Jesus—Son of God and Light of the World—bringing him into line with all the other Sun Gods of mythology born on the night of the Winter Solstice. ✳ In a similar manner, Easter, the highest holy day on the Christian calendar, always celebrates the death and resurrection of Jesus at the time of the Spring Equinox, when new life is resurrected once again from the dead cold of winter into the rebirth and warm rebirth of spring. The Jewish feast of Passover also coincides with the Spring Equinox. Carl Jung noticed, "There is no such thing as coincidence," and that could not be more true when it comes to organized religion's synchronistic timing of high holy days with nature's most divinely powerful turning points. ✳ In planning our spells and rituals, therefore, consider the divine power in nature, and pay careful attention to the seasons of the year and phases of the moon. Align the mysteries in your life with the mysterious transformations in nature and see for yourself how enchanting and sacred those moments become. What the power in nature reveals is that death is never final, but is always followed closely by some kind of new life. Even when we feel devastated by loss and death, the power in nature reveals that new life will grow there soon, some new life will appear even in the darkest and deadest of times. In the spirit world, endings are always full of magic for new beginnings, and our souls always become the phoenix, rising from ashes over and over again, into even more fullness of life. Aligning ourselves with the divine power in nature, then, always adds an extra special charge to the transforming magic in ritual.

REPETITION

Repetition is the secret of probability, according to Jung, meaning that the more times we repeat a certain activity the greater the chances of getting a desired outcome. The same truth applies to repetition's power in creating the magic of ritual. The most sacred and powerful rituals we know are those that have been repeated over and over again for as long as we can remember. It's the same as the power in a mantra. We are very careful to use the same words, the same gestures, and the same symbols, believing that each and every one bears a sacred power that builds and grows with every repetition. So much so that they indeed effect what they signify, just as they did in the beginning. ✳ Even with family rituals, extra special care is usually taken to repeat the way it was done in the beginning, the way it was done when something extraordinary first occurred. We gather the same people, on the same date, serve the same foods, do the same activities, repeating everything with the hope of recreating the closeness and joy we know every time we gather on that day, and in that way. We rely naturally on the magic of repetition to connect us with divine activity. ✳ The power in repetition is easy to understand when you think of how meaningful certain things become the more we do them. The significance deepens over time, and does so in such a profoundly simple, almost unconscious way that we find ourselves relying on such rituals for our own well-being, our own peace of mind. We even feel out of whack if we miss those times. People who belong to clubs understand this perfectly, as do most nuns I know, for whom religious life depends upon such regular, repetitive coming together. Getting together regularly for years is all it takes to transform strangers into friends, and friends into family, into sisters. Such is the divine power in repetition. ✳ For some, me included, even a day doesn't feel right if we don't do certain things. If I don't write every day, for example, I start to feel disconnected, out of touch, a little gaga. I feel the same way if I don't read the *New York Times* every morning, and watch some news. That's how much of a ritual reading and writing can become. And while I find such spiritual richness in other religious traditions, nothing moves me more than the rituals of

Catholicism that I've known and repeated for years, those same rituals that have been repeated by billions of believers for centuries. The power in repetition is divinely charged with that kind of timeless magic. ✳ Sacred words, sacred gestures, and sacred objects all play a big part in creating the power in repetition, and all become sacred from having been repeated over and over and over again. The real power in repetition is something many of us were introduced to early in life while writing 500 times "I will not talk or laugh in class"; as though writing it hundreds of times would become so much a part of us that we would naturally no longer talk and fool around while Sister was trying to teach. Similarly, the writing and copying of illuminated manuscripts has always been experienced as a sacred ritual by monks and nuns, somehow effecting in them a mystical experience. So never underestimate the power in repetition. For believers, it's everything but repetitive. ✳ Words have always been associated with the sacred, and certain words carry a power, and when repeated do indeed effect what they signify. Hearing someone say, "I love you," naturally makes us feel loved. And words of hate and anger can devastate us just as swiftly. Ordinary bread and wine become divine when we repeat the words attributed to Jesus at the Last Supper: "This is my body. This is my blood." Say but the words and the magic of ritual does its work. Miracles happen. (*Abra-*

cadabra is one of the oldest and most repeated of those words.) Because certain words are so powerful, the repetition of those words over and over has everything to do with making the magic of ritual, especially when combined with the powers in faith, necessity, and nature. ✳ Repeating certain ritualistic gestures has a similar divine effect. While praying "Kadush, Kadush, Kadush"—Holy, Holy, Holy—Jews stand on tiptoe, lifting themselves closer to heaven. By extending our hands in prayer, we bless. By anointing the forehead with oil, or by immersing in water, we bless and baptize new life. By the laying on of our hands, we heal the sick, and lift depressed spirits from their dead-feeling state. And when we fold our hands in prayer, in effect we point and focus our thoughts on the holy. Such actions, repeated for thousands of years, seem to have built up a divine power that gets tapped into and released whenever we do the same, whenever we repeat those gestures in our spells and blessings. ✳ In preparing your rituals therefore, integrate into everything you do the power in belief, necessity, nature, and repetition. In doing so, you become connected and aligned with all holy spirits who have uttered those words and offered those prayers. And once you're that connected, you're ready to begin.

HOW TO DO SPELLS
AND BLESSINGS

BECAUSE SO MUCH OF RITUAL'S transforming power comes from what we bring to the altar, there's also a method to the magic of ritual, certain steps that are good to follow whenever we engage in ritual prayer. And like all steps that are good to follow, their real goodness lies in making them our own, in making them part of the flow with which we go every time we do our spells and blessings. Far more than just an outline or a list of things to do, however, each step works in some specific way to prepare us for divine intervention, to get us ready for a visit with the Gods. So assuming that you've heard the call to ritual prayer, created sacred space, and prepared your altar, you're now ready to begin making magic. You now have all you need to begin. ✳ Taking you through the seven steps I usually go through is the best way I know to explain how these spells and blessings work. It's the only way I know to show how each step puts us more and more in touch with the mystery and magic in ritual prayer. The amount of time you spend on each step is never as important as your readiness to move on. So don't worry about timing, it comes naturally. The more frequently you engage in ritual prayer, the more attuned you become to your own rhythm, and the more comfortable you also become going with the flow. ✳ Skipping steps has never been good for me. Each works in a different way to create and deepen the magic. Each carries its own uniquely divine charge. And each makes us more and more ready to sit still with the Gods for a spell. For that reason alone, I try not to skip steps. These seven steps are not parts of ritual prayer as much as they are a process to go through from beginning to end. Step by step, each draws us gradually deeper and deeper into sacred space, into the magic of ritual, and just as gradually brings us back again, transformed. Feeling both different and the same. ✳ Not at all unlike a recipe for ritual prayer, these steps provide everything you need to whip up some divine activity of your own. Whether you engage in ritual prayer alone or in community with family and friends, keep in mind that these steps can be adapted easily to involve all who come together to pray. ✳ Keep in mind also that the more deeply involved participants are, the more powerful rituals become. Each step works to alter and deepen consciousness, increase our awareness so much that we experience ourselves and others as divine, our bodies as sacred, and everything that happens to us as blessing. All of life becomes holy when we engage in ritual prayer, and these are the steps I found to help make that kind of magic happen.

STEP ONE: CHOOSE THE DATE

While any spell or blessing can be done at any time, with no preparation other than a pure heart and a still moment, there are other times when we may want to align our prayers and ourselves with the divine powers in nature. Birthdays, anniversaries, full moons and new moons, Solstice and Equinox, all are naturally sacred times for ritual prayer. Charged as they are with the divine power in nature, all are loaded with the divine energy of transformation, the infinite potential to change the seasons of our lives also. Nature and necessity are always the first two powers to line up with whenever choosing the date for spells and blessings. ✳ Before we look to nature to select a date, therefore, choosing the day has everything to do with what we're asking for, with what we need. It also has everything to do with clarifying and focusing our wishes before placing them on the altar. First and foremost, wherever the need for a spell or blessing comes from, never is it ours to judge the merit or significance. Don't even go there. Whatever the inner necessity that calls us to ritual prayer, that's where divine activity has already begun. So never even question requests for what may look like little things—a new job, new boss, sick pet, quit smoking, lose weight—everything that comes from a sincere heart is precious in the sight of the Gods; as it should be in our sight also. ✳ Purity of heart is where we always start even before we choose the date. According to the Beatitudes, it's what we need to see God. That's how blessed the pure of heart are, they can see God. Pure how? Without any wish to harm. Without hatred and anger that want revenge. Leave your offering on the altar and make peace first is what Jesus tells us to do when we're that angry. A firm reminder to be very careful with what we ask for, and to purify requests of anything negative before we even think of approaching the altar. ✳ So if you're thinking about doing someone in, now's the time to think again. Think instead about praying that all obstacles (inside and out) be removed so that only good things happen through you, as well as those you'd like to eliminate. Think also about praying that others be bound from hurting you or standing in the way of your success and happiness. Praying to be bound by love and protected from all harm is a good way to focus any kind of anger and resentment that may accompany a request. It's the focus on healing, not hurting, that makes the heart pure enough to see God. ✳ Once the request is clear, and the heart pure, you can then decide the best time and place for your spells and blessings, you can then choose the date. In doing so, consult all calendars—lunar, seasonal, holidays, and holy days—and align yourself with all the divine powers already present there. The lunar calendar, for example, has always been a determining factor in setting the dates to mark holy days. And there's always been something mysterious and powerful about the moon's effect on us. Not only do the phases of the moon regulate ocean tides, menstrual cycles, crop cycles, and possibly UFO sightings; they also affect the ups and downs of our spiritual life as well. ✳ Many find that their intuitive, psychic energy is highest when the moon is full, making it an opportune time to focus on attracting what we want in our spells and blessings. And in a similar manner, when the moon is dark and our energy low, that becomes the most opportune time to remove any negative stuff from our life, getting all obstacles out of our way. And if we pay no attention to the moon at all, and think it has no influence on life whatsoever, some believe that causes lunacy. So take a lesson from every major religion and consult the lunar calendar when choosing the date for your spells and blessings. There's naturally magic there. ✳ Religious feasts and holy days are also perfect times for joining in with our prayer. Find the date that's most fitting for you and your wish, then work toward aligning yourself with the divine powers already present. In Catholicism, for example, not only is there a saint named as patron for every day of the year, but every illness has its protector saint, and every profession has its patron saint. Everyone and everything had a saint, it seemed, and praying for certain favors, on certain days, from certain saints, was always believed to be extra powerful. Your prayer automatically had their divine and everlasting support. ✳ All of this is to say that the more divine forces we gather to work with us in our spells and blessings, the more powerfully transforming the results. So when it comes to choosing the date, take care to align yourself with all the powers of nature available to you at the time, to connect with as much divine energy as you can. Finding the most powerful day for your spells and blessings is the very first step.

STEP TWO: MAKE HOLY THE DAY

Once we choose the date for our spells and blessings, that day naturally becomes a holy day, a day set apart from all the rest, a day in which the Gods will be stopping by for a spell. Sabbath. With that in the mind, don't be surprised if the day you choose always looks and feels different. From sunrise to moonrise, your wish becomes the focus, the moment for which you spend the day preparing. How we get ourselves and our homes ready for divine intervention has everything to do with step number two: Making holy the day we choose for our spells and blessings. ✳ If you are accustomed to participating in religious services on the Sabbath, then there is no better way to make holy the day than by engaging in those most sacred of religious rituals. Whatever you do to make the day holy, begin with a prayer of thanks, and throughout the day keep an inner focus on what it is you want to happen. Do everything you can to avoid anything negative that day. Do whatever you need to do to prepare yourself for a divine visit. ✳ In addition to preparing and collecting ourselves for ritual prayer, we also need to prepare our home and altar as well. Gather together everything you need—candles, flowers, water, stones, incense—and assemble the sacred items on the altar. The area designated for ritual prayer needs to be free from distraction, clutter, and anything else that may diminish the focus. Housekeeping is almost always part of my making the day holy, and clearing the clutter always tops the list—from mind, heart, soul, and house. ✳ Whatever you need to do to make holy the day you set aside for your spells and blessings, that's the next most important step. It's the divine matter of getting yourself and your home ready for divine activity. The day you choose becomes your Sabbath. It becomes noticeably different from all other days in that the most important work of the day is the work of your spells and blessings. ✳ So even though the day we choose may, of necessity, be full of its ordinary works and distractions, they too become part of the Sabbath, and they too can work to focus the day on the moment set for ritual prayer. The whole day works to charge us for our spells and blessings, making extra holy the moment we begin.

STEP THREE: BEGINNING

While the time to begin your spells and blessings is entirely up to you, never underestimate the power in the hour, and the mystery in the still of the night. Like the seasons of the year, some hours are more naturally charged than others, and those are the perfect times for ritual prayer. For example, there's something magical about midnight on New Year's Eve, Christmas Eve, and Holy Saturday, that's unlike any other midnight I know. That same enchanted feeling comes with the exact time spring arrives, the hour you were born, the rising of any full moon, the hour loved ones died, all kinds of anniversaries. Whatever time feels magic, that hour becomes a naturally powerful time to begin spells and blessings. ✳ For me, the power in the hour is almost always in the still of the night, around midnight, just before bedtime. Day is done, and even city life settles down. Today turns into tomorrow. And that's when nearly all my spells and blessings begin—in the still and the dark of the night, around midnight. Everything feels more mysterious at night, revealing the more enchanting side of darkness. Candles burn brighter. Clouds of incense rise thicker and higher. Moon and stars appear. And most of the world is asleep, leaving us alone in solitary splendor. Nighttime is naturally soul time. Made for prayers, spells, and blessings. Made for a visit from the Gods, who have a reputation for appearing to us at night, in darkness, in sleep, and in dreams. Night is clearly the time when Gods prefer to do their work. That's also when I prefer to do mine. ✳ If your days are as full as mine, you too may need to alter your consciousness before you begin; to shift gears from day to night, and start focusing more single-heartedly on what it is you're praying for. I do that in the bathtub. A foaming hot bubble bath does it every time. The running water. The clouds of bubbles. The steam heat. The mermaid collection. The rubber shark. Candlelight. Totally divine. I'm there. And the longer I'm there, the more ready I am to begin. ✳ While historically, there are many ways to alter consciousness for ritual prayer—meditation, yoga, alcohol and drugs, fasting—I recommend highly the natural ways, such as soaking in a foaming hot bubble bath. After that, I guarantee you will be ready to begin. But whatever way you choose to shift gears and enter sacred space, whatever you do to get yourself there, when the appointed time comes, (instinct tells you when), that's the time to approach the altar and begin.

STEP FOUR: CANDLE LIGHTING

Most of us have been lighting candles and making wishes since our first birthday. Very early in life we were introduced into the wish-come-true magic of candle lighting, and ever since it's become more and more a part of my everyday life. So much so, that whenever I light a candle, I always dedicate it to someone or something. And I light a lot of candles. Just light some candles, turn out the lights, and see for yourself how quickly the room is transformed into sacred space. That's what candle lighting does for our spells and blessings—helps create sacred space where wishes come true and prayers are answered. It signals the Gods that we are ready to begin. ✳ The lighting of candles has always been a symbol that sacred rituals are about to begin. In Biblical days, fire was a sacred symbol to express the presence of God, as it is here in the lighting of candles for prayer. In the Catholic Mass, as in most religious rituals, candle lighting is the signal that something sacred is about to happen. Something extraordinary is about to occur. The same is true here. Candle lighting signals that our spells and blessings are about to begin. In the lighting of candles, the door to the spirit world opens and the Gods become present. ✳ Because candle lighting is such a powerful moment in initiating ritual prayer, it's always good to anoint and prepare candles before lighting. Anointing objects with oil before placing them on the altar is another ancient religious tradition. Its purpose is to consecrate objects for prayer and to mark the spot of divine presence. Anoint candles by rubbing your favorite scented oil (olive oil is also fine) along the sides and top of the candle, all the while focusing on what it is you want to happen. Carving initials, dates, or symbols on the candles before anointing further enhances the ritual. In anointing with oil, we thank the Gods for all that we've been given, charge the candle with our wish, and dedicate the lighting to the answer of our prayer. ✳ So take care to prepare candles before lighting. Anoint and charge them with your spirit. Then light the candles, darken the room, and focus on the circle of light within which your spells and blessings will now be done. If others are joining you, now is the time for everyone to circle around the altar. Either way—alone or together—candle lighting signals the time that our spells and blessings have begun. Something extraordinary is about to happen. Divine intervention is about to occur. That's how powerful candle lighting is when beginning our spells and blessings. It signals the presence of God.

STEP FIVE: INCENSING

Incensing follows candle lighting in doing these spells and blessings—the burning of incense and the appearance of thick white clouds of sometimes intoxicating smoke. Just as God often spoke from fire in Biblical days, so too did God appear frequently in clouds of smoke. Mists and clouds always signified the close proximity of God, a sure sign of divine activity, so much so that incensing became the door-opener for all ancient religious rituals. Just prior to the moment of consecration in the Catholic Mass, for example, the altar, the congregation, the deacons, and even the priest himself is incensed with clouds of frankincense and myrrh. Then the moment of transformation occurs and bread and wine become divine. Incensing serves the very same purpose here. The clouds of smoke that rise from our incensing are a sure sign that God is present and the magic of ritual has begun. ✳ Practically speaking, incensing involves nothing more than the burning of smudge sticks or scented incense. Sandalwood is good all-purpose incense for rituals, as is frankincense and myrrh, church incense. Smudge sticks are little bundles of dried sage, long believed to be a sacred herb of the Gods. Sage is also the magic ingredient that makes turkey stuffing so divine. Always associated with heightening the power and mystery of religious rituals, the burning of incense or sage also works to purify the sacred space, and all those gathered within. It purifies us completely, inside and out, making us all better able to see what's really going on. ✳ It's the smoke from the incensing, like the flame in candle lighting, that's meant to be as mind altering as it is purifying. Because Gods are known to appear in clouds of smoke, breathe it all in and let it pass through you, clearing your mind and sharpening your focus. Pass the incense over and around everyone and everything present, purifying and preparing everyone for divine activity. If you are not alone, have participants incense one another. All are equal participants in these spells and blessings. Incense is the prelude to the goose-bump experience. It always sends up the signal that the Gods are now present and the magic has begun. What we want to happen has become real. Incensing marks the beginning of some enchanted evening. ✳ If you are allergic to or irritated by smoke and incense, sprinkling with holy water is just as effective in every way. Pour holy water into a shallow bowl or cup, and using a small tree branch, sprinkle everyone in your circle. You may also want to anoint everyone there with holy water: Dip your thumb in holy water, then anoint your forehead, your lips, and your heart with a sign of the cross or some other sacred symbol. Where to get holy water? From any priest, sister, or church if you practice a religion that uses it. Seawater always feels holy to me, as is, surprisingly, the water in Manhattan's East River (according to shamans from Tibet). And in the good old days, rainwater was believed to have magical power, coming as it does from heaven. Any water from sites sacred to us becomes holy. ✳ You can also, as many do, make and bless your own holy water. All you need are candles, incense, water, salt, sunlight or moonlight, and a bell. A Holy Water Blessing is included in this book (p. 77) for those who wish to make their own water holy. Whether we incense with smudge sticks or sprinkle with holy water, both are old, sacred rituals known to summon the Gods and let divine activity begin. We are at the heart of ritual's mystery now, transformation's turning point. Everything is in place for the magic to happen. It's abracadabra time.

STEP SIX: ABRACADABRA

Surrounded by candlelight, incense, the presence of Gods and holy spirits, you can now cast your spell, pray for a blessing, make your magic. This is the moment of transformation. This is when we place our offering on the altar and let the Gods do their work. Whatever spell or blessing you've chosen, now is the time to do what it says. Now is the time to make abracadabra. I usually begin solitary rituals with one of several opening prayers. Either the Memorare, or Hail Mary, old Catholic prayers to Mary, Holy Mother, an ancient prayer to the Goddess, or The Lord's Prayer, the prayer Jesus recommends. Find your own favorite prayers, your mantra, and begin all spells and blessings with prayers you know by heart. Those are your most sacred words. Those are your abracadabra. ✳ Having opened the door to divine intervention, everything we do now becomes part of rituals' transforming magic, and every move we make carries a divine charge. Anything can happen. It's the feeling of being connected, in touch, like something is really happening, what we envision is becoming real. Whatever God or divine power you call upon, whatever moves you make, whatever words you speak, whatever spell or blessing you choose, all of that now becomes charged with the magic in ritual, and all of it works immediately as it's done to begin answering our prayer. ✳ Because consciousness is so raised at this point, even the simplest gesture, like standing on tiptoe, feels deeply moving. As do such ordinary things like bread and wine. Feeling moved to tears or laughter is 100 percent normal in sacred space, so don't be surprised if your spells and blessings end up full of both. I've laughed until I cried many times. Feeling connected deeply to everything is typical of the kind of transformation we experience here, oftentimes making the atmosphere divinely social, even fun. It's as though what we're really asking for has already been granted, and for whatever reason, no one is surprised. All these mysterious feelings become sure signs of divine activity, clear indicators of the magic of ritual at work. ✳ So if you want to sell a house, or find an apartment, and you're doing the Saint Joseph Real Estate Spell (p. 99), now is the time to wrap and bury Saint Joseph. If you're doing the Happy Birthday Spell (p. 90), and it's midnight, now's the time to make your wish. In the Catholic Mass, this is the point at which bread and wine become divine. This is where we follow with reckless abandon whatever our spells and blessings call us to do. And this is where we become transformed by such divine activity, where the magic in ritual does its work of making real what we've just asked for. And even though we may not be able to see results clearly at the time, we nonetheless continue to believe, believe, believe—keeping in mind that any hesitation at all in our hearts immediately breaks the spell. ✳ Doing spells and blessings with a pure believing heart is the most powerful abracadabra of all. Here we take ordinary, everyday life, bring it into sacred space, place it on the altar, and pray that it becomes all that it can be. We pray that it becomes divine. Ends turn into new beginnings here, and peace comes flowing like a river through even our worst misery. All of life becomes sacred here, touched by God. When you've reached that divine point—after you've said your abracadabras and your work is done—don't be surprised if it's also then that you hear those words of wisdom, "Let it be," which is to say: Consider it done, now let it go.

STEP SEVEN: LET IT BE

✳ Letting it be has everything to do with how to bring your ritual to a close and what happens next. When the spell or blessing is done, let it go. You've placed it in the lap of the Gods, now let it be. Let the Gods do their divine activities. Consider it already done and never question results. Don't break the spell by hesitating in your heart. That's all it takes to do so. In its own time, and in its own way, whatever you prayed for will come to you. But between now and then, between here and there, the last step you take in doing your spells and blessings is this: Let it be. ✳ In bringing your spells and blessings to a close, I recommend doing so in the same way you began. Step out in the same way you entered. Repeat the prayer used in the beginning, the one you know by heart, adding immediate thanks for some enchanted evening. I'm not a singer, but those who are often close with a song. Candles can be extinguished now also, or left to burn. But with or without candlelight, the transformation has occurred, and whatever we prayed for is being done. All that we do in the closing of our ritual is always done in the spirit of thanks and letting it be. ✳ How to let it be? I always like celebrating a little (sometimes a lot), after a good spell or blessing. When I'm alone, even if it's after midnight, I usually have a divine little snack. I'm one of those grown-ups who sit in the dark eating Frosted Flakes, M&Ms (peanut), Swedish Fish, Cheetos. When I'm with a group, with the sisters for example, we usually have dinner or dessert afterward. And every church I've ever been to always has a social after the service. Some kind of celebration is always in order after our spells and blessings, even if you're alone. After all, we just had a divine visit with the Gods. ✳ Within four to six weeks, you should begin to see some sign of your prayer being answered. You should begin to notice that something's changed, especially your way of thinking about the matter in question. And if you are truly letting it be, you will also see clearly how strong patience makes you, how free believing it all makes you, and how much peace and joy there is to be found in drumming up divine activity at home. You may even want to further empower your spells and blessings by repeating the same ritual consecutively for three days, or weekly for four or nine weeks. Once again, never underestimate the divine power in repetition ✳ An offering of thanks is always in order at the concluding of any ritual prayer, and for me it can go on and on for days. It's only common courtesy after such a divine visit that we would offer thanks in kind. How? By becoming kinder, more compassionate, more generous. If you have spare change, give it away to anyone who asks. Take time to listen to someone else's heartache. Be more patient and accepting of those who drive you crazy. Be braver and never tolerate injustice and discrimination. Let all the divine activity of your spells and blessings bring out all the divine activity in you. More than anything else, let that be. That would be the answer to my prayer. So let it be, let it be, let it be.

SPELLS AND
*
BLESSINGS:
*
MINE

*

*

*

*

*

CANDLE LIGHTING WISH-COME-TRUE SPELL

Lighting a candle and making a wish is a little spell and blessing all by itself. It's also the perfect way to pray when that's all the time and energy you have. The power in fire and the power in heartfelt wishes make this simple spell work like magic. Nature and necessity always make magic whenever we light a candle and make a wish.

So whenever you hear even the faintest call to pray, light a candle and make a wish. And never light a candle, for whatever purpose, without dedicating it to someone or something. In a similar manner, never extinguish a candle without confirming your wish with a "Blessed be" or an "Amen." Keep in mind that every time you light a candle and make a wish you are taking part in a divine activity. You too are making magic.

BLESSED BE.

THREE KINGS HOUSE BLESSING

This blessing is done in the home every New Year, preferably on January 6, Feast of the Magi, who had an epiphany on that day. It's the most perfect time of the year to pray for an epiphany in our lives also, one of the best days for divine intervention, for blessing everything that will happen in the year to come. The focus of all New Year house blessings is on purifying the home of anything negative that happened the previous year, and on blessing the home with peace and love for the New Year.

ON THE ALTAR

PIN OR KNIFE FOR CARVING

1 WHITE CANDLE

1 GREEN CANDLE

OIL FOR ANOINTING

INCENSE

HOLY WATER

EVERGREEN BRANCH

RECORDING OF "WE THREE KINGS"

(OPTIONAL BACKGROUND MUSIC)

WHITE CHALK

1. **CANDLE LIGHTING** ✳ Before anointing, carve the year past into the white candle, and the New Year date into the green candle. In anointing the white candle, focus on and be grateful for all the good things that happened in your home the previous year, praying that anything negative be removed. In anointing the green candle, focus with gratitude on your hope for the year to come, praying for protection from all harm. Then light the candles.

2. **INCENSING** ✳ Light the incense from the green candle, allowing its smoke to rise. Then take the incense throughout the house, incensing the corners of each room (especially closets), and all around the doorways. Incense also every living person and thing. While doing so, focus on purifying your home and your life of anything negative. Return the incense to the altar and let it burn.

3. **BLESSING** ✳ Take the evergreen branch and holy water throughout the house, sprinkling and blessing the same areas that were incensed, including again pets, plants, and everyone present. While blessing with holy water, pray that your home and all who live there be blessed and protected in the year to come. When done, return the holy water and evergreen branch

to the altar. ✳ Then take the chalk, and above the doorway to each entrance write K + M + B + [current year]. Return the chalk to the altar. Let the candles and incense burn. Your house is blessed.

4. CLOSING ✳ In concluding the Three Kings House Blessing, promise to make some offering of gratitude for a healthy and happy New Year: a donation of time or money to charity, or some other proportional act of kindness. Never underestimate the divine power in gratitude and in generosity, particularly as you begin a New Year.

HAPPY NEW YEAR
BLESSED BE.

FULL MOON HOLY WATER BLESSING

This ritual is for those who do not have access to holy water from a priest, nun, or church. It's an old folk blessing used for making your own holy water, and it's always done under a full moon.

ON THE ALTAR

1 BOWL WATER

SMALL BOWL ROCK SALT

2 WHITE CANDLES

ANOINTING OIL

INCENSE

1 BELL

Place the bowls of water and salt in the center of the altar with a candle on either side.

DIRECTIONS

1. CANDLE LIGHTING ✳ Anoint both white candles, focusing on purifying your heart for the blessing of water. Light both candles, repeating your own favorite prayer.

2. INCENSING ✳ Light the incense from one of the candles and let it burn, allowing its smoke to rise. Take the bowl of water, hold it over the incense, and focus on purifying the water for blessing, repeating, "Blessed be." Do the same with the bowl of rock salt, repeating once again, "Blessed be."

3. BLESSING ✳ Take the bell and ring it 3 times over the bowl of salt and 3 times over the bowl of water. Then take 3 pinches of salt and add to the water. Extend your hands in blessing over the bowl of water, repeating Saint Francis's Canticle to the Sun. (p. 106)

4. CLOSING ✳ In closing, set the water bowl under the full moon for 3 days (day before, day of, day after). Then store the holy water in an airtight container, keeping it on the altar for your spells and blessings.

BLESSED BE.

NEW JOB SPELL

This spell is for all those who are jobless or unhappily employed. Its focus is on getting paid for work you love to do. In preparing for this spell, be very specific about what it is you're looking for. Envision yourself doing the work you love. That vision is full of real magic for this spell.

New Job Spells are best done near the full moon, on Sundays or Wednesdays.

ON THE ALTAR

5" CIRCLE OF YELLOW CLOTH

7 GOLD STARS

7 SUNFLOWER SEEDS

BUSINESS CARDS/SYMBOL OF WORK WANTED

5" GOLD CORD

YOUR RESUME

PIN OR KNIFE FOR CARVING

2 YELLOW CANDLES

ANOINTING OIL

INCENSE

Place the circular cloth in the center of the altar with one candle on either side. Put the stars, seeds, symbol, and cord in the center of the cloth, with resume nearby.

DIRECTIONS

1. **CANDLE LIGHTING** ✳ Before anointing, carve your initials on one candle, and the job you want on the other. While anointing, envision yourself doing the work you want. Light the candles and pray for a blessing. Using your own prayer is always best, or select one from here.

2. **INCENSING** ✳ Light the incense, passing its smoke over all the items on the altar. Then take your resume or job application; hold it over the incense, praying, "As I wish, so might it be." Do the same with the symbol of the work you want, praying once again, "As I wish, so might it be." Then hold your hands over the incense, allowing the smoke to pass through your fingers, praying for the third time, "As I wish, so might it be."

3. **THE SPELL** ✳ Take the parchment, and with the green pen draw a circle. Within the circle write the job and salary you

want. Fold it three times, seal it with a bit of saliva, and place it in the center of the yellow cloth. Then make your new job charm. Gather the items, tying them together in the yellow cloth. Using the gold cord, make three knots, repeating after each, "Blessed be." Place the charm on top of your resume and let it be.

4. CLOSING ✳ Before bedtime, extinguish the candles, praying, "As I wish, so might it be." Take the charm and place it under your pillow for 9 nights. If you have job interviews during that time, take the charm with you. If it's a job you want, leave a sunflower seed and a gold star behind. If not, just leave. After nine days, sprinkle the rest of the contents near the work you want. Bury the parchment near there as well. Keep the charm cloth and gold cord in a sacred place for future job magic.

BLESSED BE.

MEMORARE

This is an old Catholic prayer, known by heart and repeated by generations for centuries. It is so full of divine power that many find just repeating it bestows blessings, believe it or not.

Remember, O Most Gracious Virgin Mary
that never was it known
that anyone who fled to thy protection
implored thy help
or sought thy intercession
was left unaided.
Inspired with this confidence,
I fly unto thee,
O Virgin of Virgins, my Mother.
To thee do I come,
before thee I stand,
sinful and sorrowful.
O Mother of the Word Incarnate,
despise not my petition,
but in thy mercy
hear and answer me.

Amen.

BLESSED MOTHER BROKEN
HEART BLESSING

Whatever the cause, there are few things in life that need a blessing more than a broken heart. These are those soulful breaks that long for the kind of relief only a God can provide. That's how deep it goes. At times such as those that try our souls, the simple lighting of a candle can be a healing blessing in itself; as are old prayers, psalms, poems, and other sacred writings that hold healing power.

For Catholics, no one knows a broken heart better than the Blessed Mother (or any mother for that matter), and Catholic or not, Mary never says no to broken hearts. Hearts are hearts are hearts. This blessing calls on the Mother of God to heal our broken heart and grant our request.

ON THE ALTAR

STATUE/ICON OF THE VIRGIN MARY

3 BLUE CANDLES

1 WHITE CANDLE

PIN OR KNIFE FOR CARVING

ANOINTING OIL (ROSE IS NICE)

INCENSE

Place the Virgin in the center of the altar. In front, make a triangle with the blue candles, placing the white candle in the middle.

DIRECTIONS

1. **CANDLE LIGHTING** ✳ Before anointing the blue candles, carve the word "holy" around the center of each. While anointing, focus on all sadness and heartache being comforted. Carve your initials into the white candle, and then anoint, focusing on opening your broken heart to Mary's healing power. ✳ Light all 3 blue candles, then pray the Memorare (p. 82).

2. **INCENSING** ✳ Light the incense from the top blue candle. Hold the white candle over the incense, breathe in the smoke and focus on Mary's healing presence moving through you. Do the same holding both halves of the white felt heart, and focus on Mary's comfort surrounding you.

3. **BLESSING** ✳ Light the white candle, representing you, from the top blue candle, while repeating, "As I pray, so might it be." Then take the two halves of the felt heart and stitch them together with the blue thread, repeating with every

stitch, "Blessed be." Leave the stitched heart on the altar until bedtime.

4. CLOSING ✳ Before extinguishing the candles, or before bedtime, whichever comes first, repeat the Memorare. Place the felt heart under your pillow for nine days. After 9 days, bury the heart in a flower garden, repeating for the third time the Memorare.

BLESSED BE.

LUCKY WINNER GAMBLING SPELL

This spell really worked for a woman sitting next to me at the slots in New Orleans, and probably works just as well for church bingo. It should be done at home five minutes before departure.

Take a green candle and carve dollar signs on all sides. Light the candle, make a wish to win, let it burn for five minutes, then blow out. Rub your hands in the smoke, imagining money coming to you in whatever game you play. Don't wash your hands until after gambling. ✳ If you have more time, try the Money Magic Spell (p. 95), the Good Luck Spell (p. 166), or the Saint Anthony Miracle Blessing (p. 120). In any event, good luck.

BLESSED BE.

PROBLEM SOLVING SPELL

Nothing brings us to our senses or calls us to pray like a good problem. And religion tells us there's nothing Gods are drawn to more than those who need divine assistance. So if something happens, and you don't know what to do, then a Problem Solving Spell may be just for you. The focus is on clarity, insight, and being still enough to hear the inner voice, to listen to intuition, to let conscience be your guide. The spell is simple and should be done right before bedtime. Sleeping on it is an important part of problem solving spells.

ON THE ALTAR

PIN OR KNIFE FOR CARVING

1 BROWN CANDLE

ANOINTING OIL

INCENSE

1 BAY LEAF

PEN

DIRECTIONS

1. CANDLE LIGHTING ✳ Carve the name of the problem into the candle and anoint. Focus on receiving a message about

next steps by morning. Light the candle and repeat either Thomas Merton's Prayer (p. 89), Veni Creator Spiritu (p. 137), or your favorite prayer.

2. INCENSING ✳ Light the incense and hold the brown candle over its smoke, envisioning the problem being solved and repeating, "As I wish so might it be."

3. THE SPELL ✳ Take the bay leaf and write the name of the problem on one side, your name on the other. Place it under the candle and let the candle burn.

4. CLOSING ✳ At bedtime, extinguish the candle, praying, "Blessed be." Place the bay leaf under your pillow for 3 days. On the third day, crumble the leaf and scatter the pieces near the site of the problem. ✳ Mondays and Tuesdays are best for Problem Solving Spells, as are new moons.

PEACE.

BLESSED BE.

THOMAS MERTON'S PRAYER

Thomas Merton was a Trappist monk who died on December 10, 1968. His writings on the contemplative life are full of blessings, this prayer being one of them.

My Lord God, I have no idea where I am going.
I do not see the road ahead of me.
I cannot know for certain where it will end,
nor do I really know myself,
and the fact that I think I am following your will
does not mean that I am actually doing so.
But I believe that the desire to please you
does in fact please you.
And I hope I have that desire in all that I am doing.
I hope I will never do anything apart from that desire.
And I know that if I do this
you will lead me by the right road,
though I may know nothing about it.
Therefore I will trust you always
though I may seem to be lost
and in the shadow of death.
I will not fear,
for you are ever with me,
and you will never leave me
to face my perils alone.

Amen.

HAPPY BIRTHDAY SPELL

This spell is a great little birthday gift for yourself, or for anyone else on their birthday. And birthday spells are always best done on your birthday. So make a party out of it and enjoy.

ON THE ALTAR

LITTLE RED CHARM BAG

3 PENNIES

3 SUNFLOWER SEEDS

CHARM/SYMBOL OF YOUR WISH

FRESH FLOWERS

2 CANDLES (YOUR FAVORITE COLOR)

PIN OR KNIFE FOR CARVING

ANOINTING OIL

INCENSE OR HOLY WATER

3" SQUARE WHITE PARCHMENT

RED PEN

Place the charm bag in the center of the altar, with the items on top, and a candle on either side.

DIRECTIONS

1. **CANDLE LIGHTING** ✳ Before anointing the candles, carve your birth date on one and your initials on the other. While anointing, focus with gratitude on the best and the worst part of the year past. In lighting the candles, make your wish, repeating your favorite prayer.

2. **INCENSING** ✳ Light the incense, passing its smoke over the birthday charms and the charm bag. Or, if using holy water, sprinkle the items and the bag, focusing on clearing the way for your birthday wish to come true.

3. **THE SPELL** ✳ Make the wish. Take the parchment, and on one side, in red ink, draw a circle. Within the circle, write one word describing the best part of the year past, and one word describing the worst part of the year past. On the other side, draw a heart, and within the heart write your wish for the year to come. Fold the paper 3 times, repeating after each fold, "As I wish, so might it be." ✳ Place the folded wish, the pennies, the seeds, and your charms into the charm bag, and leave on the altar with candles burning and flowers until bedtime.

4. **CLOSING** ✳ As you extinguish the candles, repeat, "Blessed be." Place the charm bag under your pillow for nine days, repeating before sleep, "Into your hands, I commend my

spirit." After 9 days, remove the folded paper and bury where flowers grow. Scatter the seeds and pennies in front of a church or on other holy ground. Carry your charm with you or leave it on the altar, reminding you that your birthday magic is at work.

HAPPY BIRTHDAY.

BLESSED BE.

SISTERS' HAPPY BIRTHDAY BLESSING

This is a simple nun birthday blessing that takes place after the birthday dinner, around the lighting of the candles on the birthday cake. There is one candle on the cake for everyone present. Each sister takes turns lighting one candle and making a wish for the celebrant, who makes the last wish, lights the last candle, and then, after a rowdy round or two of the nun birthday song, extinguishes them all with one blow.

The making of wishes for one another when lighting candles is a divine birthday blessing all its own. Try it and see for yourself.

HAPPY BIRTHDAY.

BLESSED BE.

SAINT JUDE BLESSING
FOR THE IMPOSSIBLE

Saint Jude is the patron saint of desperate cases and impossible requests. In repeating the Prayer to Saint Jude, you join all desperate souls who have been repeating it for centuries and finding hope. That's how powerful the Prayer to Saint Jude is. Just repeating this prayer brings instant blessing.

PRAYER TO SAINT JUDE

Saint Jude, Glorious Apostle,
faithful servant and friend of Jesus,
the name of the traitor has caused you
to be forgotten by many,
but the Church invokes you universally
as the patron of things despaired of;
pray for me who am so miserable;
pray for me that finally I may receive
the consolations and the help from Heaven
in all my necessities, tribulations, and sufferings,
particularly (make your request here),
and that I may bless God with the Elect
throughout Eternity.

Amen.

MONEY MAGIC SPELL

Plain and simple, the focus of this spell is on getting money. Because few people I know have too much of it, I frequently receive calls for money spells and prayers. This is a favorite. And fun. Male or female, you get to make a doll.

Money spells are best done under a full moon.

ON THE ALTAR

GREEN CLOTH

DOLLAR BILLS OR PLAY PAPER MONEY

WHITE THREAD

3 SILVER COINS (DIMES ARE FINE)

1 WHOLE NUTMEG

6" GOLD CORD

3" SQUARE WHITE PARCHMENT

WHITE CLOTH (BIG ENOUGH TO WRAP DOLL)

2 GREEN CANDLES

PIN OR KNIFE FOR CARVING

ANOINTING OIL (EUCALYPTUS IS GOOD)

INCENSE

DIRECTIONS

1. **MAKING THE DOLL** ✳ Get some green material and cut out a little 4" or 5" cloth doll. Stuff it with dollar bills or play paper money. Stitch it up clockwise with white thread, repeating with each stitch, "As I wish, so might it be." The doll represents you, so make it as personal as you like. Place the doll, along with the coins, nutmeg, cord, and parchment, on the white cloth in the center of the altar. Set the green candles on either side.

2. **CANDLE LIGHTING** ✳ Before anointing, carve dollar signs around the middle of both candles, along with the amount you're requesting. Anoint both candles, focusing on money coming to you. Then light both candles, using the Holy Mother prayer (p. 98), the Saint Jude Blessing for the Impossible (p. 94), or your own favorite prayer.

3. **INCENSING** ✳ Light the incense from the flame of the candle, allowing its smoke to rise. Then take the doll and hold it over the smoking incense. While doing so, give it your name

(or the name of the one in need of money), repeating: "I name you_____. You will always have more than enough." Then put the doll back on the white cloth and sprinkle with gold glitter.

4. THE SPELL ✳ Take the parchment, and in green ink write down the amount you're asking for. Fold the paper 3 times, repeating, "As I wish, so might it be." Then seal it with a bit of saliva and place it back on the white cloth. ✳ Gather everything together in the white cloth and tie in three knots with the gold cord, repeating after each, "Blessed be." Leave the charm on the altar until bedtime.

5. CLOSING ✳ Extinguish the candles, using the same prayer to close that you used in opening. Take the doll charm and hide it in a dark place. Closet corners are good. Keep the charm there until money arrives. ✳ After receiving money, remove the charm, put it on the altar, and do a little Thanksgiving Spell of your own making. Bury the parchment in a flowerbed. Carry the silver coins with you in your wallet. Keep the nutmeg and doll on the altar—a reminder of your power to make money magic.

BLESSED BE.

HAIL MARY

This is an old Catholic prayer, repeated in repentance alone billions of times. A blessing in itself.

Hail Mary, full of grace,
The Lord is with thee.
Blessed art thou among women,
and blessed is the fruit of thy womb, Jesus.
Holy Mary, Mother of God,
Pray for us sinners now,
and at the hour of our death.

Amen.

HOLY MOTHER

This is an old Goddess prayer used for spells and blessings.

O Holy Mother,
to You I pray,
come and grant my prayer
this day.
All in true accord with Thee,
As I pray, so might it be
(make your request here).

Blessed be.

SAINT JOSEPH REAL ESTATE SPELL

Along with being the divine protector of peace in the home, Saint Joseph (spouse of Mary and stepfather of Jesus), also has a long-standing reputation for granting all requests having to do with finding a happy home, as well as selling an unhappy one. And silly as it may sound, this really works.

ON THE ALTAR

BROWN PAPER (BIG ENOUGH TO WRAP STATUE)

SAINT JOSEPH STATUE (DASHBOARD SIZE IS FINE)

3" SQUARE PARCHMENT

WHITE CORD

2 BROWN CANDLES

PIN OR KNIFE FOR CARVING

ANOINTING OIL (SANDALWOOD IS GOOD)

EVERGREEN BRANCH

HOLY WATER

Place the brown paper in the center of the altar, with the statue, parchment, and cord on top. Set one candle on each side.

1. CANDLE LIGHTING ✳ Before anointing both candles, carve the address of the place you want on one candle, and the place you're leaving on the other. While anointing, focus on the place you want to get (or get rid of) and pray, while lighting:

God, in your infinite wisdom and love
You chose Joseph to be the husband of Mary,
the mother of your Son.
May we have the help of his prayers in heaven
And enjoy his protection on earth.
We ask this through Christ the Lord.

Amen.

2. BLESSING ✳ With the evergreen branch, sprinkle and bless with holy water all the items on the brown paper, focusing on all obstacles being removed to buying or selling what you want.

3. THE SPELL ✳ Take the parchment and write down the address of the place you want to buy or sell, and at what price. Fold the paper 3 times, repeating with each fold, "Saint Joseph, pray for us." Tape your wish to the bottom of the statue, then wrap the statue in brown paper and tie with the cord in three knots, repeating, "As I wish, so might it be." ✳

Place the wrapped statue in a dark corner, facing the direction you want to move. While underground is preferred, closets are good for apartment dwellers who don't have basements. Either way, it should be a hidden location, undisturbed by ordinary activity. And dark. Prayers, spells, and all divine activity seem to need the dark to work their magic. Somewhere we can't see and interfere.

4. CLOSING * Extinguish the candles, repeating the Saint Joseph Prayer used in the beginning. Once your prayer is answered, remove the statue from the dark and keep Saint Joseph in the kitchen or nearby, reminding you of his power (and yours) to find and make happy homes. * Once your prayer is answered, offer a token of gratitude. A donation to the homeless or to shelters is always a divine gesture. As is passing this spell along to all that want to buy or sell a house.

BLESSED BE.

BLESSED WORKS OF MERCY

In growing up Catholic, we were all urged to do Works of Mercy. Because these works are far more typical of Gods than they are of us, each is naturally full of blessings, and each one works like a spell in itself. So whenever we do these merciful works of God, these beatitudes, God blesses us at the very same time. That's how divine it is to do works of mercy. Each acts as a spell in itself, giving us peace in its blessing. Try one and see for yourself.

CORPORAL WORKS OF MERCY

- Feed the hungry.
- Give drink to the thirsty.
- Clothe the naked.
- Visit the imprisoned.
- Shelter the homeless.
- Visit the sick.
- Bury the dead.

SPIRITUAL WORKS OF MERCY

- Convert the sinner.
- Instruct the ignorant.

- Counsel the doubtful.
- Comfort the sorrowful.
- Bear wrongs patiently.
- Forgive injuries.
- Pray for the living and the dead.

BEATITUDES

Blessed are the poor in spirit, all that's God's is theirs.
Blessed are the brokenhearted, they shall be consoled.
Blessed are the lowly, they shall inherit the earth.
Blessed are those who hunger and thirst for justice, they shall be satisfied.
Blessed are the pure of heart, they shall see God.
Blessed are the peacemakers, they shall be called people of God.
Blessed are those who suffer persecution for justice's sake,
theirs is the kingdom of heaven.
Blessed are you when they insult you
and persecute you
and utter every kind of slander against you —
Be glad and rejoice for your reward is great in heaven.

Matthew 5:3–12

LAKESIDE TURNING POINT SPELL

This ritual is based on one that took place years ago on the shores of Lake Michigan under a full moon. It was August 15, a high holy day for Catholics celebrating the Assumption of Mary into heaven. And an extra high holy day for some nuns, who profess and renew vows on that day. All in all, spiritually speaking, it was a highly charged day.

Everyone present stood at some turning point in life, all were friends, and all were about to take off in new and different directions. The focus was on blessing one another's hopes for the year to come. This blessing can be adapted to bless any kind of turning point, and is always best done under a full moon. It also makes for a powerful New Year's Eve blessing.

The blessing began at sunset with dinner on the beach. The ritual took place between dinner and dessert. At the first sign of moonrise, gears were shifted and the ritual began. A large circle was leveled and cleared in the sand, and a campfire altar was built in the center. As the fire was being built and started, others surrounded the fire with gifts from the lake—stones, shells, driftwood, lake water, a branch for blessing, and a branch for candle lighting.

For each one present, there was a white votive candle in a floatable container. One sister prepared the candles in advance, carving the initials and birth date of each before anointing. Another made shallow little tin foil boats that worked perfectly for floating. It wasn't me, so don't ask how.

Prior to getting together, everyone was asked to bring to the altar a symbol of their hope or dream for the year to come. For example, with the wild dream of moving to New York to be a writer, I brought a blank sheet of white paper. At the time it felt totally symbolic. Still does. Everyone circled around the fire with their candle and symbol of hope.

The ritual began with a song to Mary we all knew by heart—"Ave Maris Stella"—"Hail O Star of the Sea." Lake water was passed as we blessed one another, and round after round was sung until all were sprinkled and blessed.

What followed looked something like this: One by one, each took the burning stick from the fire, lit their candle, talked about their hope for the year to come, and placed their symbol of hope around the fire. After all was said and done (with great hilarity as I recall), each took their candle, made a wish, then all walked to the shore, where the candle-wish boats were set off to sea.

The blessing concluded with dessert—s'mores—under the full moon and stars. As far as I know, everyone got their wish.

BLESSED BE.

CANTICLE TO THE SUN

This is believed to be a favorite prayer of Saint Francis of Assisi, as well as every generation of devotee since. It's a perfect blessing at the beginning of the day, the end of the day, and every other time we want to offer thanks.

O Most High, Almighty, Good God,
to You belong praise, glory, honor, and all blessing.
Praised be my God, with all your creatures,
and especially our brother the sun,
who brings us the day and brings us the light:
Fair is he and he shines with a very great splendor.
O God, the sun signifies You to us.

Praised be my God, for our sister the moon,
and for the stars,
those which You have set clear and lovely in the heavens.

Praised be my God, for our brother the wind,
and for air and clouds, calm and all weather,
by which you uphold life and all creatures.

Praised be my God, for our sister water,
who is life to us,
humble and precious and clean.

Praised be my God, for our brother fire,
through whom you give us light in the darkness.
He is bright and pleasant and mighty and strong.

Praised be my God, for our Mother the earth,
She who sustains us and keeps us,
And brings forth fruit and flowers of many colors, and grass.

Praised be my God, for all those who pardon one another for love's sake,
and who endure weakness and suffering:
Blest are they who peacefully endure:
For You dear God will give them a crown.

Praised be my God, for our sister, the death of the body,
from which no one escapes.
Blest are they who die in your sight,
for death shall have no power to do them harm.

Praise You and bless You God.
We thank you and pray to serve you with great humility.

Amen.

BEST FRIENDS NEW YEAR'S EVE SPELL

This spell was put together as a New Year's Eve Celebration for a group of friends who called themselves The Secret Order of Judith. The evening included happy hours from 7:00 to 9:00 P.M., followed by part one of the spell from around 9:00 to 10:00 P.M., and a Babette's Feast of a dinner from 10:00 P.M. until shortly before midnight. At midnight, part two of the spell took place, followed by desserts, coffees, teas, cordials, the exchange of gifts, and the pure pleasure of one another's company. The spell ended shortly before sunrise.

In addition to everyone contributing food and drink, all were asked to bring three things to the celebration: a symbol of something they wanted to get rid of from the year past, a symbol of what they wished for the New Year, and gifts for the exchange. There were eight members present for this spell.

Part one took place about one hour before dinner. The host assumed responsibility for preparing the altar. In this case it was a coffee table covered with a white linen cloth, upon which were candles (one for everyone present), incense, evergreens and holly, and plenty of room for the old and new year symbols. Taking turns, each one talked about something in the previous year that they wanted to let go of, get rid of. Then they placed the symbol on the altar and lit a candle. After all was said and done, the spell was moved to the dinner table. The candles were left to burn, surrounded by the symbols of "things be gone."

Dinner was served. Shortly before midnight the spell moved back to the altar for part two, which began with a champagne toast to the new year and a round of hugs, kisses, and new year wishes at midnight. Then once again, over coffee and desserts, each took turns making wishes for the new year. The old year symbols were removed and replaced with new year symbols. After all was said and done, the gift exchange took place, the evening wore on, and the spell never ended until the circle was broken and everyone departed, shortly before sunrise.

HAPPY NEW YEAR.

BLESSED BE.

SAINT FRANCIS PET BLESSING

If you ever want to see a Pet Blessing extraordinaire, come to the Cathedral of Saint John the Divine in New York City on the first Sunday in October, near the Feast of Saint Francis of Assisi (October 4). New Yorkers bring their pets: cats, dogs, snakes, mice, lizards, birds, whatever. The Big Apple Circus sometimes brings elephants and tigers. And Radio City Music Hall brings the camels, donkey, sheep, and ox from the Christmas Spectacular's Living Nativity. Anyone can have their animals blessed at the annual Saint John the Divine Pet Blessing.

However, if you can't bring your pet to New York City to be blessed, here's a Pet Blessing you can do at home. While October 4 is believed to be the best day of the year for Pet Blessings, feel free to bless your pets as often as necessary—in case of illness, for example, or just in gratitude for the pure love and joy of their company. It's even known to quiet down big barkers and whiners. Never underestimate the power of Saint Francis to bless you and your pets with what you need.

ON THE ALTAR

PIN OR KNIFE FOR CARVING

1 BROWN CANDLE (FOR EACH PET)

HOLY WATER

PET CHARM (COLLAR, TAGS, FAVORITE TOY)

PET PHOTO

PET TREATS

THE SPELL

With the pet present, carve its name into the candle, anoint with holy water, and light. While holding or petting the animal, pray for a blessing with Saint Francis's Canticle to the Sun (p. 106). Then, using your right hand, sprinkle holy water on your pet, and over all the pet's items on the altar. Next, put the collar and tags back on, return the toy, and give your pet the treats. Get some treats for yourself also. ✳ Let the candles burn until bedtime, then blow out, rub your hands in the smoke, lay your hands on your pet, and pray, "Blessed be."

THE TEN-CENT
CHRISTMAS TREE BLESSING

Years ago I found this on an old holy card at the flea market. It cost ten cents. Every cut-down tree should be so blessed. That was my thought then, and now.

BLESSING OF A CHRISTMAS TREE

God of all creation,
We praise You for this tree,
which brings beauty
and memories
and the promise of life to our home.
May your blessings be upon all that gather
around this tree,
all who keep the Christmas festival by its lights.
We wait for the coming of Christ,
The days of everlasting justice and peace.
You are our God, living and reigning,
forever and ever.

Amen.

NEW BABY BLESSING *

This is a nondenominational baby blessing, in which newborn life is anointed, blessed, and welcomed by family and friends. It takes place as part of a celebration for the birth of your child; for example, before or after brunch, lunch, or dinner. Parents serve as priest here. They select the godparents, plan the blessing, and if so desired, call on the presence of a minister (rabbi, nun, priest, Dalai Lama) to bless the child. You can also call on the minister to provide the holy water, oil, and altar cloths. Selecting those you want to bless your baby is the very first step.

Begin preparing for this New Baby Blessing at least one month prior to the blessing date.

ON THE ALTAR

BASKET OF BLESSINGS AND WISHES

SMALL CARDS

BELL

1 WHITE CANDLE FOR EACH IMMEDIATE FAMILY MEMBER

ALTAR TOWEL

HOLY OIL

*With gratitude to Ellen Dolan and Angela.

WHITE WINE (FOR ANOINTING)

HOLY WATER

STATUE OF VIRGIN MARY OR GODDESS

ALTAR CLOTH

BABY/FAMILY TREASURES

DIRECTIONS

The mother and godmother prepare the basket of blessings and wishes. For everyone present there is a small card (business card size) with a blessing handprinted on one side, and a child's wish scribbled on the other. To prepare the cards, think of all the blessings you want your child to have—good health, sense of humor, kindness—then illustrate that word on one side of the card. Then think of the wishes you imagine your child making—toys, books, candy—and illustrate that word on the other side of the card. Put all the cards in the basket and place on the altar. Family treasures and religious items are also placed on the altar.

When the blessing is ready to begin, the mother rings the bell and gathers everyone around the altar. She stands in the center, with the father on her left, and the minister on the right. The minister lights the candles, explains what's going to happen, then begins the blessing.

The minister first calls on God, father, and mother to bless the child with their first name. With the altar towel draped over the left arm, the minister pours a few drops of oil into her left hand, and asks the father to anoint and bless his child with the given first name. Having done so, the minister lays her hand on the child's head, praying that they be protected throughout their lives from all violence and harm to body and soul.

The minister then calls on God, father, and mother to bless the child with their middle name, given in secret by the mother. The minister pours a few drops of wine into her left hand, and anoints the child on the forehead as the mother whispers the middle name in secret. (Being given a secret middle name is an ancient Goddess tradition.) The minister then lays her hands on the child's head, praying that they always be blessed with the divine love of family—mother, father, sisters, and brothers.

The minister then calls on God, father, and mother to bless the child with their family name. She pours a few drops of holy water into her left hand and asks the godparents to anoint and bless their godchild with the family name. The minister then lays on her hands and prays that the child be blessed throughout life with the loving support of extended family and best friends.

The mother then invites everyone present to bless her child.

It's then that the basket of blessings and wishes is passed. One by one, everyone draws a card, then offers the card's blessing and wishes to the baby. It's enough to make even grown men cry. After all is said and done, celebrate. Continue to eat, drink, and make merry. Before leaving, everyone blesses the child with a kiss.

BLESSED BE.

THE LORD'S PRAYER

Without a doubt, one of the most powerful prayers of all.

Our Father,
who art in heaven,
hallowed be thy Name.
Thy kingdom come,
Thy will be done
on earth as it is in heaven.
Give us this day our daily bread.
And forgive us our trespasses,
as we forgive those who trespass against us.
Lead us not into temptation,
but deliver us from evil.
For the kingdom, the power, and the glory are Yours,
now and forever.

Amen.

HOME SWEET HOME MOVING SPELL

This is a two-day moving spell that takes place the night before and the night after you move into a new house or apartment. It can also be adapted for any kind of moving from one place to another. Because everything is packed, and you're exhausted when you do this, the ingredients are simple:

ON THE ALTAR

PIN OR KNIFE FOR CARVING

1 CANDLE

HOLY WATER

1 SMUDGE STICK/INCENSE

ROCK SALT

The focus of the first night's spell, the night before you move, is on taking only good energy with you, removing anything negative. Carve your now old address into the top half of the candle, anoint with holy water, and light. Take the incense or smudge stick, light it from the candle, and carry it throughout the house, allowing its smoke to fill and purify corners, doorways, all around the windows, and over and around all the packed boxes. While doing so, bless and be grateful for everything that happened to you there. Then take the rock salt and sprinkle a few grains in the corners of all the rooms. Let the candle burn halfway, past where you carved in the address, then extinguish, praying "Into your hands, I commend my spirit."

The focus of the second night's spell is on purifying the new space of any negative leftovers from previous residents, then blessing the space to make it sacred. Carve your new address into the bottom of the candle, anoint with holy water, and light. Just as you did the night before, take the incense throughout the house, purifying the new space. While doing so, focus on all that you hope to enjoy and find in your new home.

Then take the candle and holy water into every room, sprinkling the same areas that were incensed, blessing every room, praying for the Gods and all holy spirits to move in with you. When finished, allow the candle to burn past the new address carving. When you extinguish the candle, pray, "Into your hands, I commend my spirit."

After everything is unpacked sprinkle a few grains of rock salt in the corners of every room. Rock salt is believed to serve as a psychic purifier and protector in the home. You now have a blessed home sweet home.

BLESSED BE.

SAINT ANTHONY MIRACLE BLESSING

Saint Anthony is always prayed to as the Saint of Miracles. Like Saint Jude, the desperate and hopeless are drawn to him. Repeating this prayer is believed to be so powerful that miracles do indeed happen. It is its own blessing. Another instant spell.

PRAYER TO SAINT ANTHONY

O Holy Saint Anthony, Gentlest of Saints,
your love for God and charity for God's creatures
made you worthy, when on earth,
to possess miraculous powers.
Miracles waited on your word,
which you were ever ready to speak
for those in trouble or anxiety.
Encouraged by this thought,
I implore you to obtain for me
(make your request here).

The answer to my prayer may require a miracle;
even so, you are the Saint of Miracles.
O Gentle and Loving Saint Anthony,
whose heart was ever full of sympathy,

whisper my petition into the ears of the Sweet Infant Jesus,
who loved to be folded in your arms,
and the gratitude of my heart will ever be yours.

Amen.

NINE SATURDAYS FERTILITY SPELL

While this fertility spell was put together with someone trying to become pregnant, it can be adapted to pray for fertility of all kinds—ideas, work, crops—anything you want to grow into divine life. This ritual also centers around the Virgin Mary, Mother of God, only because I grew up with the belief that Mary never turns down a woman's request to give birth.

Springtime is the most perfect time for all fertility spells, aligning ourselves with Mother Nature who wakens all sleeping seeds at that time. Some believe it's also the time that the Virgin Mary became pregnant from a visit by an angel. The Saturday you choose to begin your fertility spell should be spent preparing for such a divine visit. Full moons are also good times for fertility spells.

ON THE ALTAR

2 WHITE CANDLES

ICON/STATUE OF VIRGIN MARY

1 RED CANDLE

PIN OR KNIFE FOR CARVING

OIL FOR ANOINTING (ROSE OIL IS GOOD)

SPRING FLOWERS

SEASHELLS

7 SUNFLOWER SEEDS

INCENSE

CUP OF WINE (OR WATER)

1 EGG (RAW OR BOILED)

3 BLUE CANDLES

DIRECTIONS

1. ANOINTING ✳ Place the 2 white candles on either side of the Virgin, and the red one in front. Carve your birth date on one white candle, and your partner's birth date on the other. On the red candle, carve the date of birth should you conceive now. Anoint all 3, while focusing on the divine intervention about to occur. Place the flowers, shells, and sunflower seeds on the altar as well.

2. INCENSING ✳ Light the incense. Hold the cup of wine over its smoke, repeating, "As we pray, so might it be." Then pass the incense over all the items on the altar. Both partners also incense each other, repeating "As we pray, so might it be."

3. CANDLE LIGHTING SPELL ✳ Light the candle signifying the mother. Pray together Holy Mother (p. 98). ✳ Light the

candle signifying the partner. Repeat together Holy Mother. ✳ Light the candle signifying the child. Repeat together Holy Mother. ✳ After candle lighting, the couple shares the cup of wine, and seals the spell with the traditional exchange of the Holy Kiss, the moment of divine intervention.

4. CLOSING ✳ Let the candles burn until bedtime. Before extinguishing, pray together the Memorare (p. 82). Within seven days, take the spell remnants (candle stubs, ashes, seeds) to a river at sunset and toss them into the water, praying "Blessed be." Then every Saturday, for the next 7 Saturdays, burn a candle in front of the Virgin and pray the Memorare.

THE NINTH SATURDAY SPELL

On the ninth Saturday, repeat the ritual as done before. To the altar add one egg (raw or boiled) and three blue candles. The focus of the ninth Saturday is on thanksgiving, good health, and all obstacles being removed to your giving birth. Drawing on the power in repetition, try to repeat your Ninth Saturday Spell at the same time as the first, and repeat every gesture just as you did then; including taking the remnants to the river in 7 days.

Some personal gesture of thanks is also important at this time. Giving thanks in advance always empowers prayer further. As does praying together the Memorare.

BLESSED BE.

SAINT THERESA E-MAIL BLESSING
RECEIVED NOVEMBER 28, 2000

If you make a wish before reading this Saint Theresa novena (believed to be very powerful), your wish will come true in four days. Just E-mail it to four others and watch what happens on the fourth day.

MAKE A WISH

May today there be peace within.
May you trust your highest power that you are exactly
where you are meant to be.
May you not forget the infinite possibilities
that are born of faith.
May you use those gifts that you have received,
and pass on the love that has been given to you.
May you be content knowing you are a child of God.
Let this presence settle into our bones,
and all our souls the freedom to sing,
dance, and bask in the sun . . .
it is there for each and every one of you.

Send this to four people in the next five minutes and your wish will come true. ✳ (On the fourth day, I finished this book just like I wished I would.)

BLESSED BE.

TRUE LOVE SPELL

The focus of this True Love Spell is on finding your soul mate. And if you think you've found a possible soul mate, that too can become clear. Have a lovely time with this spell.

ON THE ALTAR

RED ROSES

6" CIRCLE OF RED CLOTH

2 ACORNS

7 ROSE PETALS

SMALL RED FELT HEART

PERSONAL LOVE CHARMS

PIN OR KNIFE FOR CARVING

2 RED CANDLES

ANOINTING OIL (ROSE IS GOOD)

HOLY WATER

SEASHELLS

3" SQUARE PARCHMENT

RED PEN

GOLD CORD

Place red roses on the altar. Put the red circular cloth in the center of the altar, and all the love charms on top (acorns, rose petals, felt heart, charms). The days of the full moon are best for love magic, especially Fridays and Mondays.

DIRECTIONS

1. CANDLE LIGHTING ✳ Before anointing, carve your initials on one red candle, and your soul mate's initials on the other. If you don't know the initials, carve a heart with your initials in the center. While anointing, focus on the love you wish to draw into your life. While lighting both candles, repeat the Holy Mother prayer (p. 98) or a prayer of your own, one you know by heart.

2. BLESSING ✳ Sprinkle holy water on the love charms, seashells, and candles. Focus on receiving the love you're looking for. If there is someone specific, envision that person as part of your life. Imagine their spirit present with you at the altar.

3. THE SPELL ✳ Take the piece of parchment, and with the red pen draw a heart big enough to write the name or qualities you seek in finding true love. After filling the heart, fold the paper 3 times, repeating after each fold, "As I wish, so might it

be." Place your wish in the center of the red cloth with the other love charms. Tie everything together with the gold cord, using 3 knots. After each repeat, "Blessed be." Leave the love charm on the altar while the candles burn.

4. CLOSING ✳ When you extinguish the candles, repeat the "Holy Mother" prayer for the third time. (Or the same prayer used to begin.) Place the love charm under your pillow for the next 9 nights, and carry it with you for the next 9 days. And for the next 9 evenings, relight the candles and keep the love charm on the altar, reminding you of its power to make love magic. ✳ After 9 days, scatter the rose petals near the one you love. Keep the other love charms on the altar, or in a sacred place, for use in repeating true love spells.

BLESSED BE.

SAINT FRANCIS PRAYER FOR PEACE

There is a prayer attributed to Saint Francis that's known to grant instant inner peace. I can attest to that. It can either be used as an opening and closing prayer for healing, get well, and antianxiety spells, or it becomes an instant spell all its own when spoken from the seat of the soul. Its power to grant peace is miraculous.

PRAYER OF SAINT FRANCIS

Lord, make me a channel of your peace,
where there is hatred, let me sow love;
where there is injury, pardon;
where there is doubt, faith;
where there is despair, hope;
where there is darkness, light;
where there is sadness, joy.
O Divine Master, grant that I may not so much seek
to be consoled as to console,
to be understood as to understand,
to be loved as to love with all my soul.
For it is in giving that we receive,
it is in pardoning that we are pardoned,
it is in dying that we're born to eternal life

Amen.

BLESSING AT THE HOUR OF DEATH*

A friend of mine works as a hospital minister, which means she spends days and nights with the sick and dying, their family and friends. This is a blessing she does when someone dies. "What better time for a blessing," she writes, "than at the hour of death."

The hidden power in this blessing is twofold. It combines the anointing rituals of ancient burial rites and the final blessing from the burial rites of nuns. Whenever a sister dies, the community surrounds her, escorts her to her burial place, and prays for the angels to come and conduct her into paradise. This blessing does the same. It provides family and friends with a way to anoint and bless the dead, a way to do their final bidding.

ON THE ALTAR

CANDLES (IF POSSIBLE, THOSE USED FOR FAMILY OCCASIONS)

OIL FOR ANOINTING (OLIVE OR VEGETABLE OIL IS FINE. ADD A DROP OF PERFUME.)

*With gratitude to Mary Feeley.

1. CANDLE LIGHTING ✳ As everyone gathers in a circle around the bed, the candles are lit, and a simple prayer is offered:

> *Holy One, we give back to You*
> *this loved person ___name___ ,*
> *whom you have loaned to us for a short time.*
> *As they have been a blessing to us in this life,*
> *We bless them now for this final journey*
> *To your eternal light and peace.*

2. THE BLESSING ✳ Each one present then anoints and blesses a part of the body with oil—forehead, hands, feet, heart. As this is done, prayers are offered as each one gives their own final blessing. Like all rituals, this is not to be rushed. Allow time for remembering, silence, laughing, and crying, maybe even singing.

3. THE FINAL BIDDING ✳ As the anointing and blessing ritual draws to a close, all offer together the ancient prayer In Paradisum:

> *Saints of God come to their aid.*
> *Come to meet them angels of the Lord.*

God of mercy hear this prayer for ___name___ ,
whom you have called from this life.
Welcome them into the company of your saints
in the kingdom of light and peace.

Amen.

MAY THEY REST IN PEACE.

BLESSED BE.

SAFE TRAVEL BLESSING

It's still a tradition in the sisterhood to bless and pray for those who travel. Which I believe is the reason why you rarely, if ever, hear about nuns being killed in travel-related accidents. The blessings and prayers of their sisters protect them. This is a simple blessing you can do for yourself or others the night before you travel.

ON THE ALTAR

PIN OR KNIFE FOR CARVING

1 WHITE CANDLE

HOLY WATER

INCENSE

PLANE TICKET (OR CAR KEYS IF DRIVING)

HOUSE KEYS

ITINERARY

DIRECTIONS

Before anointing, carve into the candle your destination as well as your home address. Anoint, light, and pray the nun prayer before a journey:

"In the way of peace and prosperity, may God, the almighty and merciful, direct our steps. And may angels accompany us on the way, that we may return to our home in peace, and safety, and joy."

Light the incense from the candle and pass its smoke over the travel items on the altar, focusing on a safe and happy trip. Then sprinkle holy water on the items as well, repeating "As I pray, so might it be." Leave the items on the altar until the following morning. When extinguishing the candles, repeat the prayer before a journey, keeping in mind that you are now surrounded and protected by angels.

HAPPY TRAILS TO YOU.

BLESSED BE.

VENI CREATOR SPIRITU

This is a prayer monks, nuns, priests, and the whole Catholic Church has been praying (and singing) for centuries. Full of divine creative powers, it's perfect for solving problems of all kinds, and is known for helping all those working in the arts. Inspiration, insight, and fresh ideas are all works and blessings of the Holy Spirit. This is the prayer that invites the Creator Spirit to come.

Come, O Creator, Spirit blest,
And in our souls take up your rest;
Come with your grace and heavenly aid,
To fill the hearts which you have made.

O Comforter, to you we cry,
O heavenly gift of God Most High,
O fount of life and fire of love,
And sweet anointing from above.

You in your sevenfold gifts are known;
You, finger of God's hand we own;
You, promise of the Father, You,
Who do the tongue with power imbue.

Kindle our senses from above,
And make our hearts overflow with love;
With patience firm and virtue high,
The weakness of our flesh supply.

Far from us drive the foe we dread,
And grant us your true peace instead;
So shall we not, with You for guide,
Turn from the path of life aside.

Oh, may your grace on us bestow
The Father and the Son to know;
And You, through endless times confessed,
Of both the eternal Spirit blest.

Now to the Father and the Son,
Who rose from death, be glory given,
With you O Holy Comforter,
Henceforth by all in earth and heaven.

Amen.

TWO-DAY PURIFICATION SPELL

Purification spells and blessings are done to transform the awful effects of some terrible experience and prepare us for new sources of life, which are sure to come. Purification Spells are best done at the time of the new moon.

ON THE ALTAR

1 RED CANDLE

PIN OR KNIFE FOR CARVING

ANOINTING OIL (VIOLET IS GOOD)

FRESH FLOWERS FOR ALTAR

PURIFICATION CHARM OR SYMBOL FOR ALTAR

2 THREE-INCH SQUARE PIECES PARCHMENT

INCENSE

RED PEN

SMALL GLASS BOWL

1 WHITE CANDLE

1. CANDLE LIGHTING ✳ On day one, use the red candle only. Before anointing, carve into the candle some symbol of what you want removed from your life (initials, dates, etc.). While anointing, focus on every bit of misery leaving your life. Light the candle, choose an opening prayer, and place the candle in the center of the altar, with fresh flowers and a purification charm or symbol, on top of one blank piece of parchment.

2. INCENSING ✳ With purification spells, you purify and incense the home as well as the items on the altar. Carry the incense through the whole house, allowing its smoke to pass over and purify everything. While incensing, focus specifically on what it is you want out of your life. I know one woman who sang "I Wanna Wash that Man Right Outta My Hair" while incensing, and it worked. ✳ After purifying your home, return to the altar. Incense the other items on the altar. Hold the red candle and parchment over the smoke, while praying the Holy Mother prayer (p. 98) or an opening prayer of your own.

3. THE SPELL ✳ Take the parchment, in red ink draw a circle, and write within it all that you want taken away (fear, anger,

depression, etc). Read aloud the items, praying after each "Be gone, blessed be." Place the parchment under the burning candle and let it be. ✳ Shortly before bedtime, take the list from under the candle, fold the paper 3 times, repeating "Blessed be" after each, then seal it with a bit of saliva. Using tweezers, hold the folded list over the candle flame to ignite, allowing it to burn in the glass bowl. As the wish burns, pray "As I wish, so might it be."

4. CLOSING ✳ When extinguishing the candles, pray "Into your hands I commend my spirit. Blessed be." Reserve the ashes and candle stubs.

DAY TWO: NIGHT AFTER NEW MOON

On the following night, repeat the spell at the same time, if possible. The focus of the second night is on what you want to bring into your life to turn it around, what it is you hope to happen. Carve into the white candle your birth date and a symbol of your hope. And on the parchment, use the red ink to specify what you want to happen now—your heart's desire. Everything else remains the same.

As soon as possible, but no later than the next new moon

(30 days), take the ashes and candle remnants to the river, toss them over your left shoulder into the water, walk away, and don't look back.

BLESSED BE.

OUR LADY OF LOURDES
GET WELL BLESSING

This is another instant spell. So powerful is the faith in Our Lady of Lourdes that countless healing miracles are attributed to her divine intervention, even today. Repeating this prayer and blessing yourself with holy water is believed to be full of healing power. The next best thing to being there. Some Catholic gift stores sell holy water from Lourdes, but your own works just as well for this blessing.

PRAYER TO OUR LADY OF LOURDES

O ever Immaculate Virgin, Mother of Mercy,
health of the sick, refuge of sinners,
comforter of the afflicted,
you know my wants, my troubles, my sufferings;
look with mercy on me.
By appearing in the Grotto of Lourdes,
you were pleased to make it a privileged sanctuary,
whence you grant your favors;
and already many sufferers have obtained
the cure of their infirmities, both spiritual and corporal.
I come, therefore, with complete confidence
to implore your maternal intercession.

Obtain, O loving Mother, the grant of my requests
(make your request here).
Through gratitude for your favors,
I will endeavor to imitate your virtues,
That I may one day share your glory.

Amen.

THREE-DAY SUCCESS SPELL

Success spells are for those who really want to excel at the work and life they love. This has nothing to do with luck, but everything to do with the cycle of life and coming into our own. This is a prayer for blessing on our work, the success of which, in some big way, is often beyond our control. In the big picture, and at that level, success is a gift of the Gods. It's God's blessing on a work well done.

Success spells are best done on Sundays, under a full moon.

ON THE ALTAR

PIN OR KNIFE FOR CARVING

3 PURPLE CANDLES

ANOINTING OIL

1 WHITE CANDLE

3" SQUARE WHITE PARCHMENT

INCENSE

SYMBOL OF SUCCESS

7 ROSE PETALS

1. **CANDLE LIGHTING** ✳ Carve the word "holy" into each of the purple candles before anointing, arranging them in a triangle on the altar. On the white candle, carve your initials, and either a word or symbol of the success you seek. Place the white candle in the center of the triangle on the parchment. While anointing, focus on all obstacles to your success being removed. Then light the three purple candles only, repeating the Holy Mother prayer (p. 98) or a personal prayer for success.

2. **INCENSING** ✳ Light the incense from the top purple candle, allowing its smoke to rise. Hold the white candle over the incense, passing it through the smoke, focusing on receiving the success you ask for. Then light the white candle from the flame of the top purple candle and place it back in the center of the triangle, on top of the parchment. ✳ Take the symbol of your success (manuscript, business card, job application, etc.), pass it through the smoke of the incense, then hold it over the flame of the white candle, repeating once again your opening prayer.

3. **THE SPELL** ✳ Take the parchment from under the white candle. Draw a circle, and within the circle, write the same

word carved on the white candle. Fold the paper 3 times, repeating, "As I wish, so might it be." Then light the parchment from the flame of the white candle, allowing it to burn with the incense. Repeat, for the third time, your opening prayer.

4. CLOSING ✴ Before bedtime, extinguish the candles, repeating, "Blessed be," after each is snuffed out. For extra power, repeat this spell for 3 nights under the light of a full moon. Reserve the remains (ashes, candle stubs, etc.) on the altar. Sprinkle in a garden or flowerbed within 30 days.

GOOD LUCK.

BLESSED BE.

SISTERS' GET WELL BLESSING

This is a simple blessing that can be done whenever two or three gather around the sick. It's an ordinary blessing among nuns and others who believe healing comes through laying on of hands and praying together. The Memorare (p. 82) is a hands-down favorite. When you pray in that way, the power in your hands is full of healing, and your touch divine. So if you want to heal your sick body or soul, or that of someone else, lay on your hands and pray for a get well blessing. The Our Lady of Lourdes Get Well Blessing (p. 143) works well here also. The thought alone makes me feel better.

BLESSED BE.

GET WELL SPELL

This spell can be done for yourself or someone else. Its focus is twofold: removing all disease from mind, body, and soul, while restoring good health and well-being. Tuesdays and Thursdays are good for get well spells.

ON THE ALTAR

5" SQUARE GREEN CLOTH

1 BLUE CANDLE

1 GREEN CANDLE

ANGEL FIGURE/SYMBOL (SMALL)

7 EUCALYPTUS LEAVES

CRYSTAL OR SACRED STONE

PERSONAL HEALING CHARM

BLUE CORD

3" SQUARE WHITE PARCHMENT

PIN OR KNIFE FOR CARVING

ANOINTING OIL (EUCALYPTUS IS GOOD)

HOLY WATER/BRANCH FOR BLESSING

GREEN INK PEN

PHOTO (IF YOU'RE DOING THE SPELL FOR SOMEONE ELSE)

Place the green cloth in the center of the altar with the blue candle on the left and the green candle on the right. In the center of the green cloth put the angel, eucalyptus leaves, crystal or stone, healing charm, blue cord, and parchment.

DIRECTIONS

1. CANDLE LIGHTING ✳ Before anointing, carve into the blue candle a word or symbol of what you want healed (pain, cancer, fear, etc), and into the green candle a symbol of what you're praying for. While anointing, focus on healing energy coming into your life. Then light both candles, and while extending your hands over the flames, pray for a blessing. The Our Lady of Lourdes Get Well Blessing (p. 143) is good; better yet, your own personal prayer.

2. BLESSING ✳ Sprinkle and bless with holy water all the objects on the altar, yourself, and anyone else present. If you have pets, it's good to have them present also. While blessing with holy water, focus on its life-giving energy moving through you.

3. THE SPELL ✳ Take the parchment, and in green ink write down your specific health request. Fold the paper 3 times, repeating after each fold, "As I wish, so might it be." Then

gather all the items in the green cloth and tie together with the blue cord using three knots, repeating after each, "Blessed Be." Leave the charm on the altar between the burning candles.

4. CLOSING ✳ Before bedtime, extinguish each candle, repeating, "Into your hands, I commend my spirit." Place the get well charm under your pillow for 9 nights and carry it with you wherever you go for 9 days. If you're doing the spell for someone else, give the charm to them and have them do the same. Or, you can place the charm on their photo and leave it on the altar for 9 days, lighting a candle there every night. ✳ After 9 days, remove and unwrap the charm. Bury the folded paper in a garden and scatter the eucalyptus leaves near an evergreen tree. Keep the other healing charms on the altar, or in a sacred place, reminding you of your power to make healing magic.

BLESSED BE.

PRAYER FOR COMFORT

The psalms are some of the most soulful, powerful prayers we know, effecting in us what they signify. Psalm 23, the Shepherd Psalm, is among the most powerful of all, full of divine comfort and peace, and a personal favorite, so much so it's a blessing all its own.

PSALM 23[1]

The Lord is my shepherd,
I need nothing more.
You give me rest in green meadows,
setting me near calm waters,
where you revive my spirit.

You guide me along sure paths,
You are true to your name.
Though I should walk in death's dark valley,
I fear no evil with you by my side,
Your shepherd's staff to comfort me.

You spread a table before me
as my foes look on.

[1] *The Liturgical Psalter*, Archdiocese of Chicago: Liturgy Training Publications, Chicago, IL. 1995.

You soothe my head with oil;
My cup is more than full.

Goodness and love will tend me
Every day of my life.
I will dwell in the house of God
As long as I shall live.

BLESSED BE.

LOVE YOUR ENEMY BINDING SPELL

If someone is making your life miserable, and you want them to stop, then a binding spell may be in order. The focus is on preventing enemies from hurting you, others, and themselves, as well as protecting you from their meanness. Binding spells work for the greatest good of all and harm none. This spell is one of the best ways I know to love your enemy.

ON THE ALTAR

3 WHITE CANDLES

1 BLACK CANDLE

3" SQUARE WHITE PARCHMENT

1 BAY LEAF

PIN OR KNIFE FOR CARVING

ANOINTING OIL (EUCALYPTUS IS GOOD)

INCENSE/CENSER

BLACK PEN

Arrange the three white candles in a triangle on the altar, with the black candle in the center. Place the parchment and bay leaf under the black candle.

DIRECTIONS

1. CANDLE LIGHTING ✳ Before anointing the white candles, carve the word "holy" into all three, then anoint with eucalyptus oil. Before anointing the black candle, carve the name of the person you want to bind from making your life miserable; then anoint with eucalyptus oil. Light only the three white candles when you begin, praying the Saint Francis Prayer for Peace (p. 131).

2. INCENSING ✳ Light the incense, allowing its smoke to rise. Take the black candle and hold it over the incense, letting the smoke pass over. Do the same with the parchment and bay leaf, repeating with each, "As I wish, so might it be."

3. THE SPELL ✳ Light the black candle from the top white one. Hold the lit black candle over the incense, then using the name of your enemy, repeat, "I bind you from doing harm to others and yourself." Then place the black candle back in the center of the triangle. ✳ Take the parchment and pen. Draw a circle of protection on the paper with your name in the cen-

ter. Fold it 3 times, repeating with each fold, "Blessed be." Hold the folded parchment over the incense, then light it with the flame from the black candle, repeating again, "I bind you from doing harm to others and yourself." Let the parchment burn with the incense. ✳ Take the bay leaf and write on it with the black pen the name of your enemy. Hold it over the incense, then over the flame of the black candle, repeating once again, "I bind you from doing harm to others and yourself." Then light the bay leaf from the black candle, and let it burn in the censor. Let everything be until bedtime.

4. CLOSING ✳ After extinguishing the candles, repeat the opening prayer. Reserve the candle remnants and ashes on the altar for 7 days. Within the next 30 days, take the remnants to a river, throw them over your left shoulder into the water, repeating once again, using their name, "I bind you from doing harm to others and yourself. Blessed be." ✳ Binding spells are best done on Tuesdays and Saturdays, under a new moon.

BLESSED BE.

GUARDIAN ANGEL PROTECTION BLESSING

It's never too late to believe that a guardian angel is assigned at birth to everyone by God. The sooner the better, I think. Being surrounded constantly by such holy spirits is a real comfort in life; especially early in life, at bedtime, when right after being told not to "let the bedbugs bite," we said the first prayer we ever learned.

ANGEL OF GOD

Angel of God,
my guardian dear,
to whom God's love,
commits me here.
Ever this night (day) be at my side,
to light,
to guard,
to rule and guide.

Amen.

For as long as this prayer has been prayed by children (and adults), it naturally carries its own blessing. Put angels on your altar and keep in mind their protective presence in your life. All angels are messengers of God, so every now and then, light a candle and listen.

BLESSED BE.

DAY OF THE DEAD BLESSING

The Days of the Dead are October 31, November 1, and November 2. Halloween (All Hallows Eve and Wiccan New Year), All Saints' Day, and All Souls' Day. Days when the veil between the seen and the unseen, the living and the dead, is exceptionally thin. Hardly there at all. That's how close they are.

For those who believe in life after death, it's the time when dead friends and relatives come back for a visit. They wander around for three days of visiting and partying under the full harvest moon. It's then also that we're called to acknowledge their presence, honor them, and pray for their blessing. Those who live in Mexico and New Orleans understand the dead better than any other place I know. That's where I learned about celebrating the days of the dead.

The blessing consists of making an altar honoring dead friends, relatives, and favorite saints. Include photos, items that belonged to them, even their favorite food and drink. Anoint and burn a white candle for each, calling on them to bless you with their presence. And believe me, they will.

However you remember the dead in your life, doing so on these three days is extra powerful. The veil between us is so thin. So trick and treat yourself by celebrating the days of the dead every year. Let yourself be blessed by the loving presence of your dearly departed. Not to mention that of all the angels, saints, and everyone else wandering around in the afterlife. Acknowledging and honoring their presence is not only full of blessings, it's also a lot of fun. See for yourself how alive our dead ones really are.

BLESSED BE.

SISTERS' MEMORIAL BLESSING

Another more ordinary way to honor our dead loved ones is to remember them every time we come together. Nuns do this all the time—speak about our dead sisters, and to our dead sisters, as though they are still alive. Which they are, believe it or not. Whenever we come together that always happens. Our rituals begin by acknowledging those sisters who have died. Then from that point on, they become present. There's nothing bizarre about it at all. In remembering them, the dead naturally become present, making the sadness over loss and the joy over everlasting life nearly equal. And I don't need to explain what an infinite blessing that is.

So whenever you get together with family and friends, acknowledge the presence of your dearly departed loved ones. Remember them. Tell stories about them. There's magic in those memories in that those who are gone become present to us in a way that feels totally real and nothing short of divine. So whenever you come together, do so in memory of them. See for yourself what extraordinary blessings lie in precious memories, and feel for yourself how quickly sadness turns into its sister joy. Believe it or not, the dead are still with us. Guardian angels each and every one.

BLESSED BE.

BEGINNING OF THE
MONTH RETREAT SPELL

Retreating for a day at the beginning of every month is an old tradition among nuns that I wish was an old tradition in the world. For me it turned into one of the most divine days of all, even now. A day off from work of any kind. Doing nothing but reading, letter writing, maybe a film festival (videos), always a spell. The focus of this spell, done at the beginning and end of the day, is on blessing the best and worst times of the month past, and opening yourself more fully to the best and worst of the month to come. In this spell we pray for a blessing on it all.

ON THE ALTAR

SYMBOL OF THE BEST PART OF THE MONTH

SYMBOL OF THE WORST PART OF THE MONTH

2 WHITE CANDLES

3" SQUARE PARCHMENT

FLOWERS

PIN OR KNIFE FOR CARVING

ANOINTING OIL

INCENSE

CENSER

Place your best and worst symbols in the center of the altar, with a candle on each side. Place the parchment and flowers there also.

DIRECTIONS

1. CANDLE LIGHTING ✳ Before anointing, carve the month past into one candle, and the new month in the other. While anointing, focus on the best and worst parts of the previous month. Light the candles, praying Veni Creator Spiritu (p. 137).

2. INCENSING ✳ Light the incense, allowing its smoke to rise. Hold the lit candle on the left (past month) over the incense, focusing on blessing and purifying the best and worst parts of the month. Repeat, "Blessed be." Then hold the candle on the right over the incense, praying for a blessing on the month to come. Repeat, "Blessed be."

3. THE SPELL ✳ If safe, let the candles and incense burn through the day. The whole retreat day becomes a spell—a day of divine activity—among which, for me, is the listing of the 10 best and worst parts of the past month. If you keep a journal, a book of your days, read through the past month and see what you find there. ✳ Identify the best part of the month, and

write it in a circle on one side of the parchment. Then identify the worst part of the month, and write it in a circle on the other side of the parchment. Find a symbol of both and place in the center of the altar, between the candles. Let it be.

4. CLOSING ✳ Shortly before bedtime, fold the parchment 3 times, repeating with each fold, "Blessed be." Light the parchment from the flame of the candle on the right (new month), and let it burn in the censer. While it burns, repeat, "Veni Creator Spiritu." Then extinguish the candles, repeating, "Into your hands, I commend my spirit." With that, day is done. ✳ The following morning, sprinkle the ashes in a garden or flowerpot.

BLESSED BE.

SAINT ANTHONY FIND SOMETHING LOST SPELL

Another power attributed to Saint Anthony the Miracle Saint is that of finding lost items. The older you get, the more you may have to rely upon Saint Anthony to do that for you. There are two little prayers to Saint Anthony known to point us in the direction of lost items. My mother swears by the first, as do millions of other believers. However, both do the trick. Focus on the lost item while repeating over and over seven times:

Dear Saint Anthony,
Please come round.
Something's lost
And can't be found.

or

Saint of the lost,
Who may not stay nor stand
While one child wanders
From their mother's hand.

BLESSED BE.

GOOD LUCK SPELL

It often seems as though good luck is something totally beyond our control. Some have it and some don't. Contrary to that opinion, however, there's a lot more to good luck than meets the eye. Because according to Jung "There's no such thing as coincidence," the focus of good luck spells is to align ourselves with those connections that put us in the right place at the right time; the place where good luck always happens.

If your life is in need of some divine connections, then this Good Luck Spell might work for you.

ON THE ALTAR

1 VIOLET PLANT

1 YELLOW CANDLE

GOOD LUCK CHARMS

PIN OR KNIFE FOR CARVING

ANOINTING OIL (VIOLET IS GOOD)

INCENSE

HOLY WATER

5" YELLOW CIRCULAR CLOTH

GOLD CORD

Place the violet plant in the center of the altar, in front of the candle. Surround the plant with good luck charms.

DIRECTIONS

1. **CANDLE LIGHTING** ✳ Before anointing, carve into the candle a good luck symbol, your initials, and your birth date. Anoint with violet oil (believed to have special properties to attract good luck), focusing on opening your life to being in the right place at the right time. Then light the candle, and in your opening prayer make your wish.

2. **INCENSING** ✳ Light the incense, passing its smoke over the candle and good luck charms. Focus on all obstacles being removed to good luck coming your way.

3. **THE SPELL** ✳ Make your lucky charm. First, sprinkle the items with holy water, repeating, "As I wish, so might it be." Then gather everything together on the cloth and tie in 3 knots with the gold cord, repeating after each knot, "Blessed be."

4. **CLOSING** ✳ Extinguish the candle, repeating, "Into your hands, I commend my spirit." Place the good luck charm under your pillow at night. Carry it with you when you leave the house. At all other times, leave it on the altar, reminding

you of its power (and yours) to be in the right place at the right time.

GOOD LUCK.

BLESSED BE.

HAPPY ANNIVERSARY BLESSING

Any anniversary is a powerful day. Something life-changing happened on that date, making it naturally full of divine activity. A gift from God. This is a ritual that can be done (alone or together) to celebrate any anniversary. And because anniversaries are so personal, it's up to you to improvise for the special occasion. The focus of all anniversary rituals is on connecting us to the magic moment that first made the day into an anniversary. That's the moment we celebrate, and that's the blessing we pray for.

All anniversaries are holy days, so even if you have to work, keep an inner eye on the magic of the day, and the celebration to come. Create an anniversary altar and place there symbols of the occasion you're celebrating. It's a day to wallow in the magic of the anniversary moment. In the morning, offer thanks and prepare to receive the blessings of the day; at night celebrate and be grateful for the blessings received. Anniversary meals and parties are naturals for divine activity, as are solitary rituals, or those where two or three gather to celebrate.

Anoint and light some candles. Burn some incense. Call to mind the magic anniversary-making moment, make some wishes, and pray for its continued blessings—among which is living happily ever after. So celebrate all the anniversaries in your life. Each one is full of divine blessings.

HAPPY ANNIVERSARY.

BLESSED BE.

ANOTHER FIND
SOMETHING LOST SPELL

Take a 3" square piece of parchment and write down a description of the lost object. Right before bedtime, take a pin, anoint your fingers with oil, and stroke the pin 7 times, each time repeating the name of the lost item. Then take the paper, pin it under your pillow, and repeat the Saint Anthony Find Something Lost Spell (p. 165) 7 times. Some report finding the lost item the following day.

BLESSED BE.

ANXIETY BE GONE SPELL

There are few things in life worse than dreading or being afraid. Both prevent us and everyone around us from living happily ever after. This is a spell to get rid of those things we dread and fear. A ritual focused on removing all obstacles to inner peace and freedom, to the great calm of Buddha. Any time is a good time for anxiety spells, especially Thursdays, and particularly under the influence of a new moon.

ON THE ALTAR

5" CIRCLE OF BLUE CLOTH

2 BLUE CANDLES

PIN OR KNIFE FOR CARVING

ANOINTING OIL

INCENSE

3" SQUARE WHITE PARCHMENT

BLUE PEN

BAY LEAF

ROCK SALT

HOLY WATER

GOLD CORD

Place all items (except water, oil, and pen) on the blue cloth in the center of the altar, with one candle on each side.

DIRECTIONS

1. CANDLE LIGHTING ✳ Before anointing, carve into the candles that which you dread and fear. Anoint the candles, focusing on what life would feel like without all the anxiety. Then light the candles and pray for a blessing. Suggestions: Saint Francis Prayer for Peace (p. 131), Prayer for Comfort (p. 152), Saint Jude Blessing for the Impossible (p. 94), or a personal favorite.

2. INCENSING ✳ Light the incense and pass its smoke over the items on the altar. Hold each candle over its smoke, repeating, "Be gone. Blessed be." While incensing, envision all dread and fear being gone from your life.

3. THE SPELL ✳ Take the parchment, and with the blue pen draw a circle. Within the circle write down what you dread and fear most. Fold the paper 3 times, repeating after each fold, "Be gone. Blessed be." Place the paper on the blue cloth, cover it with the bay leaf, then sprinkle with rock salt and holy water. ✳ Then gather everything together in the blue cloth and tie with gold cord in 7 knots, repeating after each, "Blessed be."

5. **CLOSING** ✳ When extinguishing the candles, repeat the opening prayer. Place the charm under your pillow for 9 days and nights. Before the next new moon, take the charm to the water, toss over your left shoulder, and don't look back. If you're not near water, bury in a flower garden.

PEACE BE WITH YOU.

BLESSED BE.

AN IRISH BLESSING

May the blessing of light be with you—
light outside and light within.
May sunlight shine upon you and warm your heart,
'til it glows like a great peat fire
so that strangers may come and warm themselves by it.

May a blessed light shine out of your two eyes
like a candle set in two windows of a house,
bidding the wanderer to come in out of the storm.
May you ever give a kindly greeting to those
whom you pass as you go along the roads.

May the blessing of rain
—the sweet soft rain—
fall upon you
so that little flowers may spring up
to shed their sweetness in the air.
May the blessings of the earth
—the good, rich earth—
be with you.
May the earth be soft under you when you rest upon it,
tired at the end of the day.
May earth rest easy over you when at the last you lie under it.

May the earth rest so lightly over you
that your spirit may be out from under it quickly,
and up, and off, and on its way back to God.

BLESSED BE.

THANKSGIVING SPELLS AND
BLESSINGS

After all is said and done, being grateful for whatever happens is so important that it deserves a spell and blessing all its own. And what better way for you to begin making your own *Book of Spells and Blessings* than that of saying thanks. Only you can be thankful for what you receive. And really, truly saying thanks can only come from you. So when it comes to saying thanks, a spell or blessing is always in order.

It's a good practice to express thanks before and after every ritual, to be grateful for such divine activity, even though we may have no idea what really happened. Do a work of mercy in gratitude. Make a donation of time or money. Be kind to strangers. Give your spare change to anyone who asks. Becoming a grateful person is the focus of thanksgiving spells, and the spirit of generosity is its blessing. May you and those around you be full of both.

THANK YOU.

BLESSED BE.

SPELLS AND

*

BLESSINGS:

*

YOURS

*

*

*

*

*

MY SPELLS AND BLESSINGS

*

*

*

*

*

*

MY SPELLS AND BLESSINGS